WESTERN
MEMORIES

© Noodle Books and Mike Jacobs 2015   ISBN 978-1-909328-21-1

First published in 2015 by Kevin Robertson under the **NOODLE BOOKS** imprint
PO Box 279 Corhampton, SOUTHAMPTON SO32 3ZX

www.noodlebooks.co.uk

Printed in England by Berforts Information Press.

INTRODUCTION

This store of recollections principally revolves around the glorious Great Western as I knew it. Every now and then, however, other perhaps interesting railway snippets which have Great Western connections appear briefly on the stage of remembrance, and I make no apology for this. After all, the Great Western was something of a life-moulding influence on much of the world around it, and the world which it served. That, I suppose, is something to do with what "greatness" truly is.

As ever, my thanks for their help with this work go to the publisher, Kevin Robertson, for his support and unwavering enthusiasm, and to my friend, Ed McNeil, who acts, I suppose, as a highly valued and helpful sort of English language Jiminy Cricket for me. I am deeply indebted to both gentlemen. The vast majority of illustrations in the book have never been published before. Many are from my own collection, but I am grateful for the work of others which are included.

I hope that this memoir might appeal a little to anyone who has ever had any leanings towards the GWR and its successors. If it does, and if it gives enjoyment, I am glad.

Mike Jacobs
Fleurance
Gers
France

April 2015

All unaccredited views were taken by the Author.

Front cover - *Push-pull fitted 64xx No 6430 on the Yeovil Junction / Yeovil Pen Mill shuttle.*
(NB collection)

Rear cover - *"Warship" class B-B D814 "Dragon" emerging from Parson's Tunnel between Dawlish and Teignmouth with a down express. 18 July 1964*

Frontispiece - *Ranelagh Bridge turntable and servicing point just outside Paddington. No 6016 'King Edwatd V' takes priority on the turntable over Nos. 6976 'Graythwaite Hall' and 5993 'Kirby Hall'.*
(NB collection)

Opposite page - *Clanking its way through Oxford, 'R.O.D' No 3016 has charge of a long unfitted freight.*
(Henry Meyer)

Above - An undated view of Platform No 1 at Paddington and a scene which changed little from the 1930s through to the 1950s. A Birmingham / Wolverhampton service is being made ready for departure. Passengers NOT customers abound, as do the facilities to occupy them whilst waiting or prior to departure. 'Quick lunch' meant either rapid service or a sandwich, it would become corrupted to 'fast food' for the next generation. Porters (remember them?) abound and whilst the fashion for hats may not be visible smart casual was the order of the day. Photographer unknown.

Opposite - 'King' No 6018 'King Henry V1' passing the TPO (travelling Post Office) pick up point at Maidenhead with the 'Torbay Express' 6 August 1960.

WESTERN
MEMORIES

There can be no doubt that the great Western Railway *was* very special. It was, by far, the longest-lived private main line railway company in the kingdom, and spent most of its life offering a dividend to its shareholders. Readers will need no reminding of its great pedigree – developed over the years on the foundations that Isambard Kingdom Brunel and Daniel Gooch had given it – and a largely distinguished history, which included fine engineering, both mechanical and civil, and the monumental broad gauge. It maintained a fleet of stylish locomotives of individual design and had a generally incredibly loyal and committed staff. The railway also functioned in some delightful parts of the United Kingdom, as well as many areas which were, perhaps, less than delightful, but interesting, nonetheless.

I was brought up with the notion of the Great Western's specialness. My father had used it for holiday travel to the West Country in the 1920's and 1930's, and although he was no dedicated railway enthusiast, he recognised something that was great when he came across it. As children, he regaled us from time to time with tales of the Great Western as he had known it. There was much talk of the grandeur of Paddington. Also featured was the West of England Travelling Post Office which was the workplace for a time of one of his uncles who was a sorter, and who was full of tales of rushing through the night picking up and dropping the mails without stopping, including an exciting account of what happened when one of his colleagues forgot to return the equipment used to collect and drop the mail to its rightful place in the train after delivering and receiving the satchels of post at Taunton, so it was said, and the consequent high speed damage and sound effects of the devices as they encountered items of line-side furniture. Father enjoyed travelling on the Great Western as a young man holidaying in Devon and Cornwall, using the "Cornish Riviera" express (non-stop to Plymouth) and other west country bound trains, with occasional dining en route in restaurant cars, which sounded unbelievably exciting and sophisticated.

The principal tale about the latter was one which I often asked father to repeat because of its element of humour. Travelling in the same restaurant car as my father on one of his journeys was a blimpish, apparently ex-military gentleman, who in no uncertain terms demanded that the steward bring him a whiskey and soda. In those more dignified days there was no such thing as soda in a bottle, and the whiskey was delivered to his table in the company of a soda siphon. After being thanked cursorily the steward went about his business, and the blimpish one picked up the siphon to add the soda to the whiskey. At that very moment the train lurched as it crossed some points at speed and the squirt of soda was diverted into the gentleman's lap. There was a certain amount of chuntering, and the gentleman tried the siphon once more just when the carriage rocked again. The result was the same as before. By now furious, the blimpish one demanded service in a tone of voice which suggested that the mishaps were all the fault of the steward, and asked him curtly to add the soda to the whiskey. "Certainly, Sir" said the steward, picking up the siphon and

expertly administering the splash of soda without a drop being spilled. The steward bowed his head slightly in the direction of the gentleman and returned to his duties. "Hrmph! Bloody clever-dick" chuntered the gentleman towards the steward's retreating back. Father may not have been much of a class warrior, but he delighted at the debunking of pomposity.

Amongst other appetising tales of pre-war Great Western trips to the west were descriptions of the delightful summer passage of the main line beside the Exe estuary, along the sea wall to Dawlish and Teignmouth and onwards by the river Teign. And there were constant references to the red soil of South Devon. To a child surrounded by the post-war austerity of England, these glimpses of earlier and brighter times seemed like the stuff that dreams were made of, and living in chalky south Hampshire the red soil seemed a little impossible.

My first travel on the Great Western was from Paddington to South Devon, although I was rather too young to remember it, and the few details that are available were part of family lore. It was 1943, we were living in London, and my father was to spend three months convalescing at Salcombe, accompanied by his widower father and the rest of the family. The train which took us from London was, apparently, an overcrowded ambling war-time express,

which deposited us at Newton Abbot towards the end of a dull and rainy afternoon where a fairly lengthy wait ensued for the local train which would take us on to Brent, there to take the branch train to Kingsbridge, where, presumably, we would get a 'bus to Salcombe. Newton Abbot Station in the rain was evidently not a very exhilarating place to wait (actually, it still isn't!) and insult was added to injury when grandfather tried without success to buy some cigarettes from the refreshment room. He was always a man prone to grumpiness, and after being informed bluntly that there were no cigarettes to be had – "there's a war on, you know, sir", which was probably code for "regulars only, so hard luck" – he spent some time stalking up and down the platform repeating "Newton Abbot, you can have it!"

The first knowing manifestation in my life of the red soil of south Devon came about in some primary school artwork. I drew and painted trains whenever I could, and in one juvenile attempt which I actually entitled "Great Western near Newton Abbot" (childish writing and ill-spelt) the only brown which I had access to was more Red Indian than Burnt Sienna, and so the land which surrounded the train (locomotive green with a bright yellow safety-valve cover) actually turned out to be coloured very closely to what it should have been! Of course, I knew nothing about it, really, and "Newton Abbot" was merely a name which featured in family reminiscences.

Glorious Devon. From Dartmouth (the location where there was a station but never any trains) looking across the River Dart to Kingswear. A 4-6-0 is engaged in shunting the carriage sidings: an increasingly rare scene when this view was taken, 9 September 1963.

2

I had made my first remembered acquaintance with Great Western locomotives and chocolate and cream coaches when we lived in Southsea towards the end of, and just after, the war. These were to be seen on trains from Cardiff or Reading that terminated at Portsmouth and Southsea, and the locomotives were, I think, "Hall" class 4-6-0's or 4300 class 2-6-0's. As I have recounted elsewhere, it was one of these which gave me my first footplate visit when I was about four[1]. A little later, after we had moved to the, then new, Council housing development north of Portsmouth at Paulsgrove, I was able to observe them en route to and from Fareham, and to absorb more about their shape – tapered boilers, copper-capped chimneys and brass safety-valve covers. In spite of the austerity era, the latter two were still nearly always polished.

As the years progressed so I acquired more experiences of Great Western things. We lived in Middlesex and North London for a couple of years or so in the early fifties, and although there were visits to various London termini and trips from and around the metropolis, the Western Region, as it was by then, hardly figured. For a short time we lived reasonably close to Northolt Junction, where the Great Western and Great Central Joint line began, which I briefly visited, and where Western activity seemed fairly limited, at least for my short stay. Uxbridge Vine Street received transitory attention on another occasion. It seemed a little dark and quiet, and was inhabited by a simmering GW tank of some description with a short passenger train. As far as I can recall, Paddington was visited only once and this was to bid farewell to my brother when he departed to Worcester for National Service in the summer of 1954. I remember little of the detail, but I was very struck by the grandeur of the place and the bustling hordes of people.

Towards the end of that year we moved to the Isle of Wight for the remainder of the 1950's, but the separation from the mainland did not mean complete separation from Western things, and my knowledge increased through personal trips to various destinations on the mainland, and excursions organised by my school. Through the former there were visits to Oxford, which I noted as being busy and where there was plenty of activity by ex-GW steam locomotives. Didcot Motive Power Depot, now the home of the Great Western Society's Railway Centre, looked enticing, but was passed too quickly for much to be seen. A trip to Southampton in 1957 yielded the splendid sight of the beautifully restored "City of Truro" on her daily revenue-earning returning working, when she was not otherwise occupied, from Didcot to Southampton Terminus. This vision left a lasting impression of what the old Great Western must have been like.

The school Railway Club of which, of course, I was a keen member, had a yearly trip to a place of railway interest, and in the summer of 1958 we visited the Western's Old Oak Common motive power depot. For some reason our permit for the visit hadn't arrived when we made our journey, and I

A hot 20 August 1949 at Cosham finds a former LSWR 4-4-0 in charge of a through service from the WR en-route to Portsmouth. The WR coach W3508, is freshly repainted. Could that also be a bridal bouquet tied to the door handle of the second compartment? (Denis Calender)

1. "Memories of Southern Railways", published by Noodle Books in 2011.

This time it is No 5956 'Horsley Hall' which is seen at Fratton with LSWR stock in tow on the 2.45 pm Portsmouth to Reading. The 'British Railways' lettering but in GWR style on the tender will be noted.

(Denis Calender)

was detailed to pick it up from the general offices which at that time bordered Paddington's number one platform. During my brief visit to these exalted corridors I was delighted to notice a few things from times past on the walls, including a nameplate from the broad-gauge locomotive "Lord of the Isles". Old Oak Common was interesting enough, with its four turntable building, and it was good to be able to inspect some ex-Great Western power at close quarters. I remember being particularly impressed by the bogie of the "King" class engines, made all the more imposing by the outside bearings of the leading axle.

Another school excursion was a November 1958 trip to Stratford-upon-Avon to attend a performance by the Royal Shakespeare Company, and which, therefore, took those travelling on the special train into Western territory north of Basingstoke and onwards to pleasant Great Western places like Moreton-in-the-Marsh and beyond, where there was a fleeting glimpse of Adlestrop Station (shades of Edward Thomas, which pleased some pupils with poetic leanings). I have two particular memories of the four-track section between Reading and Didcot. The first was on the outward journey whilst we were travelling on the down slow line; we

were passed by a "Warship" diesel hydraulic working an up express at speed – a green streak heading a train of chocolate and cream tail of coaches which seemed to pass in a flash. The second and supremely exhilarating image was on the return journey. We were again travelling on the slow line, this time in the "up" direction, but our speed was pretty good because the engine crew was trying to make up time after an earlier locomotive failure. We were slowly overhauled by a London bound express headed by a "Castle" 4-6-0. It was like a splendid tracking shot in a film. First came the locomotive, green livery and bright work glistening in the light from our carriage windows, then a view into the cab where the driver's eyes were focused on the road ahead and the fireman was busy stoking, with the light from the open firebox door reflecting off the billowing exhaust, and then the string of coaches, it goes without saying in chocolate and cream, passengers relaxing, conversing and reading, the restaurant car with diners being attended to by white-uniformed stewards, more coaches, and finally the brake second, with the guard's profile silhouetted by the dimmer illumination of his domain.

The following year, 1959, with school in its last summer term, work had to be considered, and after unsuccessful attempts at various things I acquired a job grandly entitled "Clerical Trainee" with Imperial Chemical Industries at their Slough paint factory. Despite the humble nature of the appointment, there had to be a number of visits to the plant for interviews, medicals and so on, and to the surrounding hinterland in search of somewhere to live. These various journeys, which served to give me a more intimate view of Western things, all necessitated trips down the line from Paddington, always by suburban diesel multiple units, some still rather new, and all of which were busy with traffic. Although there were trains enough on the service, as someone virtually born and bred on the Southern, it seemed to me that the Western still hadn't truly got its head around the business of intensive suburban services. The notion of "regular interval" departure times, for example, was apparently only loosely applied to timetables and I always had a feeling at this time that had the Southern people been in charge there would have been far more local and middle distance trains to a far wider range of destinations.

Observations on these journeys included a satisfying number of original GWR railcars, whose individual design was still impressive, including express parcels car W34W. There was always the full range of ex-GWR express steam locomotives, added to on one trip by three "Britannias" all noted at Paddington at the same time. The station pilots here were still drawn from a variety of 0-6-0PT's, usually 5700's, 9400's and 1500's. Noteworthy on one trip was the sight of 5700 class No 9569 at Old Oak Common still wearing the initials "GWR" on its tanks – over eleven and a half years after nationalisation.

Things finally fell into place, and for the next couple of years or so Maidenhead was to be the place of residence, and Slough was to be the place of work. There was also to be plenty of time and opportunity to observe the local railway scene.

North British "Warship" class A1A-A1A diesel hydraulic No. D602 'Bulldog' rattles through Slough with a down express in July 1959. On the right the diesel unit is on the Windsor shuttle.

Above - "Britannia" class 4-6-2 70029 "Shooting Star" brings a down South Wales express through Slough. Identification is not helped by the headboard having been deliberately turned around, although the '7' at the start of the reporting number does indicate this to be a South Wales service.

No 3846 running along the up fast line at Iver with a steam crane. (Paul Hersey collection)

3

The weekend before I was due to start work saw me ensconced in a flat on the outskirts of Maidenhead, and even here, well away from the nearest station, I found a connection with the Great Western. A fairly long retired couple lived in the apartment upstairs. The husband had, I think, spent years being something in the City, and during the course of conversation I probed him about his commuting experience as a younger man. I was regaled with information about non-stop trains from Windsor, where the gentleman lived in those days, to Paddington, and various other suburban services. My interest was really aroused, however, when he mentioned that as a young child he could just remember the broad gauge. Unfortunately, probe as I might, no details were forthcoming.

At this time it was still possible to get a good flavour of how the Great Western used to be. For years after nationalisation the succeeding Western Region seemed to stalwartly maintain a degree of independence, whose origins doubtless sprung from former times. The last steam locomotive built to a pre-nationalisation design was a GW 9400 class 0-6-0PT delivered by the Yorkshire Engine Company (sub-contracting to Hunslet) in 1956. The same time, when there

was a general livery change throughout the whole nationalised system, Great Western chocolate and cream was reinstated as the coaching stock colour on Western Region expresses. The WR was also the region which managed to paint a wide variety of locomotives – not simply express types – in the standard Brunswick green livery, which was very close to the GWR's old colours. The Western, of course, had to have truck with diesel power after the publication of the British Railways 1955 modernisation plan, but alone of all regions it maintained a policy of developing machines using hydraulic transmission, and this continued right into the 1960's. A number of us were glad to see that when the "Western" class locomotives were introduced in 1961 the centre axles of the bogies sported outside frames, which seemed something of a nod in the direction of the "King" bogie. There were also many other lingering signs of the old Great Western, including the almost ubiquitous lower-quadrant semaphore signals. At the time of my move to Maidenhead the GWR flavour was, pleasingly, to last a few more years yet.

I suppose that I should have spent the weekend prior to my embarkation on a career as a Clerical Trainee reflecting

Busy times at West Ealing. A 61xx 2-6-2T is on westbound stopping service, destination, Slough, Twyford or Reading, whilst approaching on the left is an auto service off the line from Greenford. (Paul Hersey collection)

The exterior of Marlow station, September 1959.

upon and honing the potential skills that I would need to exercise in this exalted role, and about how I should prepare myself for service in the cause of paint manufacture, but I'm afraid I didn't. My maps and timetables tempted me with Marlow, which was the terminus of the little branch from Bourne End, and which was only just over five miles away. I took the 'bus to Marlow, and was not disappointed when I found the railway, being highly delighted to find plenty of Great Western flavour still extant on a branch line this close to London. A single platform, goods yard, cattle dock and a small locomotive shed with coal stage and water tower were all there, together with a private siding serving a large timber yard. And to cap it all, simmering gently in the platform was grubby 1400 0-4-2T No 1447 with a push-pull trailer. Although she had over four years life ahead of her, she looked shabby enough to give the impression that she was fairly close to the end of her days, and had no shed plate although she must have been based at Slough. Maybe she had no British Railways shed plate, but amazingly she still sported the 1934-42 GWR roundel, sometimes irreverently referred to as the "shirt button", on her tank sides.

So taken with Marlow branch was I that I visited the station

again the next day, and learned as much as I could about the place, aided by the booking clerk, who may have found my enquiries something of an antidote to the Sunday slowness of business. His office still had a range of GWR tickets for lesser used journeys, including a three monthly season blank, and he also told me when I enquired about freight traffic, that on one day the previous week there had been eighty-two revenue earning wagons in the goods yard. How different things were from the "basic railway" which still serves the town today.

On both days I travelled back to Maidenhead on the train. The short trip from Marlow to Bourne End was a delight, with glimpses of the Thames and across the valley there was a view of what Jerome K Jerome in his splendid "Three Men In A Boat" described as the "sweetly pretty" Quarry Woods. At Bourne End I changed from the push-pull "Marlow Donkey" (as it was known by many locals) to trains from High Wycombe at Bourne End. These were reasonably well patronised, and were headed by 6100 2-6-2T's or 9400 0-6-0PT's.

The day after my second visit to Marlow was the day when I had to face up to the needs of work, and for a time thereafter I became a rail commuter from Maidenhead to

Opposite - *The station at Bourne End as seen from the footbridge in September 1959. Straight ahead the line continues to Maidenhead whilst the Marlow branch and its associated bay platform are on the right. The passengers are waiting for a train from High Wycombe.*

INTERLUDE at MARLOW

Circa 1960 Austin Attewell visited Marlow to record detail around the station. At the time the facilities provided catered for both passenger and goods, whilst some signs of the past were still present in the form of the 'cordon' gas tank wagon. In these views the auto-train has arrived and the engine has uncoupled - probably to take water at the small shed in the background. (Continued overleaf - ...)

Marlow was still handling some goods, primarily parcels traffic at this time, notice the various items piled up against the end of the station building and seen in the view lower left. Otherwise it is the motor-car which is dominant and no doubt a reasonably well patronised station Café.

1400 class 0-4-2T No. 1435 on the Marlow push-pull potters in Furze Platt Halt (north of Maidenhead) to collect one lady passenger. 27 August 1961.

Above - *The water tower and locomotive shed (sub to Slough, 81B) at Marlow, September 1959.*

Left - 1400 class 0-4-2T No 1445 leaving Marlow on the 11.20 am through service to maidenhead, 17 February 1962. Locally the branch train was known as the 'Marlow Donkey'. (Leslie Sandler)

Slough. The whole change of life took a bit of dealing with. My clerical traineeship found me immersed in largely rather boring work in the ICI Paints Distribution Department. "Distribution" briefly raised some hopes of dealings with the railway, but I soon discovered that at this time ninety eight percent of all our products found their way to their destinations by road. As with a brief period of my primary school life when I had trains passing outside the classroom window, a saving grace was the location of my base. The Distribution Department on the ICI campus was to be found in a building right next door to the Paddington main line with good views of all the comings and goings, and this was an unexpected bonus. To take the edge off somewhat, those of us who worked in the place often remarked on the fact that on the south side we had the railway, with its attendant locomotive exhaust, on the western side was a busy main road with plentiful traffic fumes, to the north was the varnish plant, constantly liable to emit the odd burst of noxious fumes, and on the east was the Slough gasworks, which was a proper traditional coal consuming plant and therefore generally rather smelly. Added to all this, the building which was our workplace was, I think, mainly clad with asbestos panels, and most of us smoked as well, so perhaps it is a wonder that any of us survived at all!

It wasn't only the Great Western main line which passed the windows. Between the slow lines and our workplace there was a line which branched off the up slow track to the east of Slough station, and which gave access to our neighbour, the gasworks. It split into two just beyond our window, one track being used for the delivery of coal supplies, and the other for storing empty wagons prior to their collection. To enable the movement of wagons to take place, the gasworks had its own shunting locomotive, a tiny green "Planet" diesel, which trundled noisily past our windows two or three times a day whilst it sorted things out. Slightly east of us, another short siding branched from those serving the gasworks and finished alongside a goods platform which served the ICI works, and where around eight or nine vans were loaded every week. Most days, as I remember, a 5700 class pannier tank propelled wagons into the sidings, and collected empties from the gasworks, and sometimes loaded vans from us, at around 10.30a.m. every morning. Shunting was a very ponderous process, accompanied by slow exhaust beats, which gave plenty of time for the more youthful members of the locomotive footplate crews to peer through our windows and smile at the younger female staff.

The goods platform line at ICI was the final vestige of what had once been a complex arrangement of sidings serving the plant. One of the skills I learned fairly early on in my clerical traineeship was that of wandering about, and a clip-board and purposeful expression enabled access to be gained to many parts of the works. It wasn't long before I discovered the disused remains of sidings which ran almost as far as the Slough branch of the Grand Union Canal which was virtually our northern boundary. The points and lengths of track which once connected them with the remaining

solitary siding were removed in February 1960, and the loading platform became the last evidence of rail transport into and from the plant. I think that at this time something like eighty tons were despatched by rail on average each week, and much of this was waste material. Occasionally more exciting things happened, such as in early 1960 when a number of SNCF ferry vans arrived to take away some stuff for export.

For the couple of years that I worked there the constant watching of the scene through the office windows, sometimes at the expense of what I should have been doing, gave a good all round idea of the daily fortunes and workings of the Great Western mainline, and from time to time unusual and interesting things were to be seen as well. Early on in my tenure, for example, in October 1959, the Brown-Boveri gas turbine locomotive ordered by the GWR before nationalisation and numbered 18000 by BR passed on two consecutive days with a semi-fast up train, returning later in the day with a west-bound express. Another lingering piece of the Great Western was also evident once a day, and this was the rapid passage of an up express featuring double tail-lamps, the time-honoured indication that a rear coach had been slipped at an intermediate station, in this case, I think at Didcot, the last example of slipping on the West of England main line. Somewhat later, the slip coach itself appeared, worked in a Paddington-bound semi-fast train. I remember it as a version of a Hawksworth coach of post-war design finished in standard BR maroon, with large vacuum brake cylinders slung under the frames, and word "SLIP" painted at each end, along with the prominent warning bell and deep observation windows for the guard. Slip coaches had been abandoned on all other British lines a long time previously, and the GWR was the only company which continued with their use, reintroducing them after World War II. I think that the Didcot service ceased in the spring of 1960, and the final example of slip coach working ceased in September of that year when the late afternoon train from Paddington to Wolverhampton, which had slipped a coach at Bicester for years, had a stop inserted into its schedule to replace the slip.

October 1959 also saw rather new North British diesel hydraulic B-B's D6306 and D6307 heading west with milk empties, and a few days later the English Electric experimental 0-6-0 diesel electric shunter D0226, resplendent in black livery with a wide orange stripe along its waistline, ambled in the same direction with a handful of wagons.

Regular sightings during this period were newly constructed Class 4 "Warship" express diesel hydraulics on running-in turns after out-shopping from Swindon, and in the following year, their new North British sisters appeared on the same workings. Towards the end of October 1959 I noted "Warship" D812, as yet un-named, and in works primer with the number painted on at one end only, on this duty, but still emitting the characteristic whistling and rattling

Slough Estates Hudswell Clarke 0-6-0ST No 3 shunting at the western end of the Trading Estate. 2 July 1960.

Slough Estates Hudswell Clarke 0-6-0ST No 3 shunting the exchange sidings at the western end of the Trading Estate. 2 July 1960.

5700 class 0-6-0PT shunting the yard at Maidenhead. 19 September 1961.

Single unit railcar W55015 rests at Staines West before returning to West Drayton. 16 July 1960.

57xx Pannier tank No 5766 passing Bourne End on coal empties from High Wycombe to Maidenhead.. 17 February 1962. Local freight continued to use the line north of Bourne End until July 1966 and it was subsequently closed completely from 4 May 1970. (Leslie Sandler)

Left - The interior of the Guard's compartment of a slip coach. The slipping lever is alongside the screw handbrake. Just visible to the left of the handbrake is the pedal for sounding the warning bell. A seat was provided behind the small partition. (BR)

Right - The Guard checking the special lamps provided on the rear of the slip portion. (S W Baker)

noise of this type – lack of paint there might have been, but clearly good mechanical condition there also was – proceeding rapidly towards Paddington.

In my early days of servitude at ICI the procession of passing trains was largely steam-hauled, mainly by ex-Great Western types. It will be gathered from the observations already written that as the months passed there were increasing diesel inroads, both on express and local workings. As with everywhere else during this period, freight traffic was usually the last to succumb, and our neighbouring railway was no exception, 2-8-0's and mixed traffic 4-6-0's still making frequent appearances.

An interesting variant from the more commonplace was the twice daily appearance of the ex-GW Parcels Railcar W34W. These workings ceased in January 1960, and were replaced for a few days by an ex-GW passenger railcar with a four-wheeled general utility van in tow. Then in February a brand spanking new BR Gloucester R C & W motor

parcels van in immaculate olive green livery took over the turn - further evidence of the constant changes of this period. Around this time I noted a number of occasions when BR Standard 0-6-0 diesel shunters were included running dead in up goods trains, presumably en route from servicing or construction at Swindon to their revenue-earning work.

There was a pleasing diversion from the ordinary in April 1960 with the stately progress west of the preserved Caledonian Railway 4-2-2 No. 123, bursting with energy, towing the GWR 4-4-0 "City of Truro". A brake van was marshalled between the two. The locomotives had been on exhibition at Westbourne Park, and were heading for their next public appearance at Oxford. Their dignified progress and immaculate appearance brought a large percentage of the population of the office, most of whom had no interest in railways, to the windows, and when I happened to mention that "City of Truro" was probably the first human-created machine to exceed a hundred miles an hour, a colleague,

The "South Wales Pullman" arriving at Paddington. The sets were not numbered as such although the individual vehicles were. Motor brake second No 60094 is leading. A small destination blind to advise passengers if it were a South Wales or Birmingham service was provided between the guard's door and engine compartment louvers, 5 September 1963.

On the same day, a further example of how the Western Region had moved rapidly towards dieselisation. 'Hymek' B-B diesel No D7010 leaving Paddington with a parcels working.

who was a committed and enthusiastic biker and always searching for an opportunity to do the legendary "ton", said sceptically and a little sniffily "What? That old crate did 102 mph? Never!" I remember one lady member of staff observing "They're so much prettier than what we've got today....." Actually, I think that the biker might have been a bit of a closet railway enthusiast, because the previous month, prompted by a newspaper item reporting the completion at Swindon of the last BR steam locomotive, 9F 2-10-0 "Evening Star", he'd quietly commented to me "Bloody shame. The end of an era."

The sighting of "City of Truro" and no. 123 heralded a day of contrasts. Later in the afternoon one of the splendid London Midland Region Blue Pullmans tore by, heading westward for a reason unknown. Perhaps it was some kind of proving run. The Western was to receive its own (eight-car) version for its prestige trains, "The Bristol Pullman" and "The Birmingham Pullman" which started later in 1960. A "South Wales Pullman" using the 'spare' set came soon after. Streamlined high speed units, with power cars at each end, these were a real break with tradition. Did we but know it, they were to be the progenitors of the ground breaking 1970's HST's, which owed some of their features to developments made from some aspects of the Pullmans. It might be said that the HST's were casting their shadows long before they became realities.

Later in the year, with my team leader's permission, I quietly played truant from my workplace to witness and photograph the first working of the down "Bristol Pullman" passing through Slough station. The train slipped through at a cool eighty miles an hour, but I did not feel particularly stirred by the experience. Grandeur – and the blue and white colour scheme was rather grand – and innovation were less and less accompanied by mechanical pomp and fireworks. When I returned to my desk my team leader came over. "Saw the new train out of the window. I know it was blue, but aside from that it looked just like any other train to me." He looked at me and shook his head gently. I have a feeling that he thought I was slightly barmy.

Parcel car W34 taking the Greenford line at West Ealing. Such was the continuing demand for vehicles to cater with this type of traffic into BR days that some modern replacements were introduced in the 1950s. The hefty buffer stop will be noted - necessitated due to previous incidents perhaps? In the background the two grounded huts show distinct similarity to standard wooden signal-box structures. (Paul Hersey collection)

3

From the autumn of 1959 to the winter of 1961 I got to know the Paddington to Reading section of the Great Western mainline pretty well, and acquired an acquaintanceship, sometimes more than a nodding one, with the branches connected with it. I also became familiar to a greater or lesser extent with many of the industrial installations in the area which used the railway, and which provided an extra layer of interest.

There were countless visits to Paddington, and it is hard to believe that, in spite of diesel railcars and shunters, and the original A1A-A1A North British "Warships" together with the increasingly ubiquitous B-B variety, there were still many steam locomotives to be seen. Although it was clear that this state of affairs was not going to last, looking back on it the sheer number and variety of types that were at work in mid-1960 seems amazing. In one trip of short duration from Maidenhead to Paddington and back, I noted well over seventy steam engines of eighteen different classes. At this long distance in time, when there tend to be only memories of change and decay, it is good to be reminded that things were not always as black as memory sometimes suggests.

I enjoyed many visits to Reading, and, whilst not completely ignoring the ex-Southern Railway Reading South Station (I was, after all, still a Southern man at heart), spent many enjoyable hours surrounded by the usually busy activity of the Great Western's Reading General. There was a constant procession of passenger trains, express, local and inter-regional at the platforms, and the regular plod of freight trains, most of which seemed to use the un-platformed lines to the north of the station. Hardly ever was there a dull moment, and there was always the chance of special traffic, such as those trains laid on for Newbury Race days.

On my arrivals from Maidenhead there was always a little locomotive activity at the Southern's motive power depot, and at the nearby late-lamented Huntley and Palmers biscuit factory their spotless royal blue 0-4-0 fireless shunter was nearly always to be seen. On the other side of the tracks there was the Great Western's extensive goods yard at a lower level, with its inclined connection to the main line to the east of the station, and a sharply curved single line, which burrowed sinuously through the embankment which supported all the GW tracks, to connect with the Southern. The connection used by all workings, other than freight trains with business in the GW yard, was situated at a respectable distance to the east of the Station, and was laid out to enable running between the two systems at reasonable speeds. With its ten platforms, including bays for trains terminating or starting, Reading General was, indeed, always a station to be reckoned with, and to a great extent remains so today, despite the fact that the goods yards, the Southern's station and depot, and Huntley and Palmers plant

This page and opposite. Interior views of one of the initial batch of GWR diesel railcars and of the type which incorporated a buffet. As can be anticipated only limited seating capacity was available and yet these vehicles were still to be seen being used on the occasional Paddington to Reading service until finally withdrawn. (Paul Hersey collection)

Reading shed with some of its usual compliment of steam present. Visible are examples of the 'Castle', 'Hall', '57xx' and 'Prairie' types. The lifting shop is alongside whilst beyond is the main line: identified by the forest of semaphore signals. With the end of the steam the shed was demolished and replaced by a diesel-depot. This saw service for over 40 years until the site was cleared and will now form part of the course of the flyover for the Berks and Hants line into Reading station. (Paul Hersey collection)

Crossing from the down relief on to the down main line by Reading East signal box. On the left is the Southern engine shed and in-between a GWR engine on the gradient connecting the two railways. Clearly re-ballasting at least has been taking place on the up main line.
(Paul Hersey collection)

have all been destroyed and replaced by redevelopments which render the old sites unrecognisable.

The point on the mainline nearest to where I lived was at White Waltham, to the west of Maidenhead. It was on that stretch of Brunel's brilliantly nearly level track which runs for miles mostly in a shallow cutting, frustratingly disallowing much in the way of views of passing scenery for passengers in trains. There was, of course, no station here, but at that time White Waltham possessed a small goods yard on the down side of the fast tracks and a refuge siding on the up side of the slow lines. These and the associated crossovers were governed from a signal box. The goods yard served local customers, presumably at one time including the adjacent Airfield, originally the property of De Havilland and then owned by the RAF, as Headquarters of the Air Transport Auxiliary Service from 1940 to 1946, and inhabited also by Fairey Aviation. During my time Fairey Aviation was still developing and testing its impressive, if noisy, *Rotodyne* gyroplane, which sadly never came to anything, at White Waltham, and which I witnessed in flight a couple of times. The *Rotodyne* outlived the railway facilities, which went in 1960, but not for too long, and

nowadays trains thunder obliviously by the site where there is now no trace of either the refuge or the goods facility.

As remarked earlier, I became familiar with the branches with a passenger service which left the main line between Paddington and Reading. There was the busy Windsor line, with the touch of faded royal grandeur to be found at the terminus at Windsor and Eton Central, and the Twyford to Henley branch which at the right time of year really did enjoy jolly boating weather and seemed to reflect it. Some may find it a little curious, but I found the branch from West Drayton and Yiewsley to Staines West more interesting than the others in a quirky sort of way when I made its acquaintance in the summer of 1960. The branch had been dieselised, and I made the trip on WR Gloucester R C & W single unit railcar W55015. Setting off from the bay platform at West Drayton which it shared with the ex-GW diesel railcar working the Uxbridge Vine Street branch, we skirted round the north of the goods yard and then headed south, burrowing under the main line. The branch's goods service had been curtailed by then, and there was no freight south of Colnbrook, the principal intermediate station, where I noted a 9400 class 0-6-PT undertaking some

Through working from Kingswear. An unidentified member of the 'Hall' class London bound in what can only be Sonning Cutting east of Reading. (M W Earley)

East and West at Reading.

For over 100 years Reading station changed little - that is subsequent to the time when Brunel's 'one-sided' station design was consigned to history. In the 21st century however almost all of the GWR influence was finally obliterated, replaced a new-age concrete, glass and stainless-steel monolith. Sights such as this, both train and infrastructure, have finally been consigned to history. **Above** - No 6959 'Peating Hall' approaching from the direction of Didcot with a stopping service. **Left** - Looking east towards Twyford and London. A steam hauled express approached whilst the DMU from which the view was taken, awaits departure from the bay on a stopping service. April / May 1960.

Above - West Ealing milk yard with 61xx 2-6-2T No 6132 taking water after its run from Kensington milk yard. At the same time 'Hall' No 4950 'Patshull Hall' passed on the up slow line with a stopping service from Reading. 29 December 1961.
(B H Jackson)

Left - No 5008 'Raglan Castle' at speed through Hanwell with a West of England working.
(C R L Coles)

leisurely shunting. As the name of the latter settlement implies, for most of its length the line followed the valley of the Colne Brook, a tributary of the Thames, and served housing estates through incredibly closely spaced stations. The first was Colnbrook Estate Halt, two and three quarter miles from the start of the journey, followed in rapid succession by Colnbrook (three miles) Poyle Estate Halt (three and a quarter miles) and Poyle, for Stanwell Moor Halt (three and three quarters of a mile). We paused at all these, and passengers were forthcoming. Further on there was Yeoveney, which I recorded as a tumbledown wooden platform in overgrown surroundings (stop on request). Clearly there was no such request, and we rattled through and past its undergrowth at a good pace.

The territory the branch line served could have been described as fairly tame, but was a comfortable far cry from pre-Tudor times when the proprietors of the "Ostrich" inn, set in what was those days were the wilds of "Colne Brook", had devised an ingenious system for accommodating, and then murdering and robbing travellers who stayed at their establishment. All we had to contend with in 1960 were the housing estates, and preliminary work on the M5 motorway which necessitated an un-gated level crossing for construction traffic. Like all intriguing railways, however, it had its unlikely charms. There was a half-cultivated, but overgrown garden at Colnbrook. On the face of it nothing much charming about that, perhaps, but the charm was conveyed by an enormous number of tall and highly colourful hollyhocks which brightened its dereliction. The

wartime connection between the Great Western branch and the Southern's line from Windsor was still *in situ*, but buried in weeds, and I particularly liked Staines West Station. This was an adapted Georgian gentleman's house which had been bought from a mill owner by the line's promoters, the Staines and West Drayton Railway, to save money, and which became its southern terminus in 1885. Even when I first visited, however, things were on the decline. The once extensive goods yard had had its connection with the branch severed, and an unused water tower stood rusting and solitary at the entrance to the station platform.

Passenger traffic was good, and all the intermediate stations, except, of course, Yeoveney, yielded people who rode the train. These were mainly women, mainly young, some with 'prams and pushchairs, who may have been heading for, or returning from, a shopping spree in Staines, if such a thing were possible. A jovial conductor guard issued tickets from a rack not dissimilar to those that used to be used by some 'bus companies (he did not have a bell-punch machine, though). He clearly knew many of the passengers and talked with them as a friend, and helped them with the 'prams and pushchairs. Passengers were not the only traffic. Freight may have been largely discontinued, but there were parcels to load and unload at Staines West, and revenue earning traffic on that day included two baskets of pigeons.

I also developed more than a nodding acquaintance with the whole of the erstwhile Aylesbury Railway. I was already familiar with its southern end from my previous trips

The end of the working weekend. '61xx' 2-6-2T No 6152 heading a Maidenhead bound permanent way train pauses at Cookham to allow a ganger or two to alight. 19 June 1960.

Former GWR diesel railcar, W31W prepares to leave West drayton and Yiewsley for Uxbridge (Vine Street). Behind is the modern equivalent, Gloucester RC&W single unit railcar W55015 on the Staines West service. 16 July 1960.

between Bourne End and Maidenhead, and I tended to patronise it using my nearest stopping place, Furze Platt Halt, for journeys over its full length, northwards to High Wycombe and on to Princes Risborough for the final portion to Aylesbury.

On my first visit, I noted that High Wycombe was quieter that I was hoping that a mainline station would be. There seemed to be little traffic, and this was borne out by the train I took onwards to Princes Risborough – lonely and lightly-loaded corridor brake second W2226W, hauled by 0-6-0PT 5420.

I was not altogether unfamiliar with Princes Risborough on paper. Curiously, whilst at school some years earlier undergoing mock and actual GCE examinations in geography, two important Great Western stations were featured on sections of one inch Ordnance Survey maps issued to we examinees to check our ability to read maps. Weston-super-Mare, with fascinating glimpses of the line of dashes symbolising "track of old railway" which gave a glimpse of the late Weston, Clevedon and Portishead Light Railway, featured in the mock exam, and the real event presented us with Princes Risborough, hitherto unknown to me, but on paper looking very tasty, with the GW & GC joint mainline, and the branches to Watlington, Oxford and Aylesbury. Regrettably, initially the first impression formed

by the map was not confirmed in actuality. My notes remind me that I recorded the place as having an "Irish" atmosphere. This was long before I had any first-hand experience of the emerald isle, and my impression was probably based on photographs of deserted railway locations in doubtful weather. Certainly on this day I was offered a vista of a lowering sky over a mainline with two fast tracks and two stopping lines bordered by wide platforms, with bays for the branch trains, with the whole picture peppered with an assortment of semaphore signals, both upper and lower quadrant, most of which remained obstinately in the "on" position for most of my visit.

The 6400 0-6-0PT headed Aylesbury branch push-pull came and went a couple of times during my sojourn, bearing with it a mere handful of passengers and the odd parcel or two. On its second visit it was joined in the up bay by another push-pull, this time from Bicester and featuring an apparently run-down 5400 and an elderly wooden-panelled trailer. I was amused, but also somewhat saddened, to observe that the control wire between engine and trailer was held together with a piece of string. I thought it confirmed that certain things were not what they used to be, and that the run-down of the old style railway was well under way.

Later on, when I came to know the place better, I came to like its occasional busy spells, especially on summer

An unidentified 'King' class 4-6-0 rushes through Princes Risborough and climbs towards the Chilterns with an up express. 28 August 1961.

Disturbing the peace. 'King' class 4-6-0 No 6014 'King Henry V11' rushing through Princes Risborough with a down express. 26 August 1961.

...meanwhile at the north end of the station, 61xx No 6138 arrives at Princes Risborough with the branch train from Thame and Oxford.

14xx class 0-4-2T No 1421 at Cookham with a train for Marlow. 17 July 1960.

Saturdays with increased GW express traffic. I believe that towards the end of the GC semi-fast services from Marylebone, Princes Risborough could have been one of the last places in the kingdom where one might regularly see main-line locomotives from three of the big four companies at work in the gathering twilight of their days.

Since the nineteen-twenties one of the things that Slough had been famous for was its trading estate. This was the first, or one of the first, of such things, which are nowadays generally referred to as "business parks". It had originally been planned as a maintenance depot where army road vehicles from first war battlefronts were to be repaired before their return to active service. It was opened in a great hurry in 1918, but its intended purpose was largely defeated by the armistice, and it pursued a somewhat unhappy career as a centre for the repair and sale of ex-army vehicles until 1925. The site was then acquired by the Slough Estates Company, and was later expanded to become the home of many businesses housed in a motley and somewhat random collection of factories and warehouses. The expansion came in for some adverse comments, and it is said that John Betjeman's well known 1937 poem "Slough" expressed his sadness and disapproval of the project and its effects.[2]

The railway had always played an important part in the life of the Trading Estate, although this was diminishing when I knew it. The whole of the Trading Estate was penetrated by its own railway system, which connected with the Great Western mainline west of Slough station, many of the plants having their own siding accommodation, and the Slough Estates Company had its own locomotives. Not long before my arrival in the area, there was a regular shuttle service of passenger trains from the bay at the west end of Slough station into the Trading Estate for those who worked or had business there. This service ceased in 1956.

At the beginning of July 1960 I made an exploratory Saturday visit to the Trading Estate, entering the territory from Burnham station at the extreme western end. I immediately came across Slough Estates No. 3, a 0-6-0ST built by Hudswell Clarke in 1925 shunting vigorously outside Weston's biscuit factory. This little locomotive was quite fun, and had a steam-operated bell which clanged incessantly all the while she was on the move. She was single-manned, and pretty clean. Pleasingly, when rail activity in the Trading Estate ceased in 1973, she was saved by the Slough and Windsor Railway Society, and now has her home on the Swindon and Cricklade Railway. Leaving No. 3 to her shunting devices, I wandered along the tracks

2. Perhaps the best known lines of the poem, and doubtless those most disliked by some Slough residents, are the first three:
"Come friendly bombs and fall on Slough!
It isn't fit for humans now,
There isn't grass too graze a cow."

through the Estate. There was still much evidence of the original owners with long stretches of flat-bottomed rails laid on base-plates cast with the W↑D symbol. There were many sharp curves, and that the track was very uneven in places.

Sometimes it was hard to tell where property boundaries were, and I remember ambling along one line and inadvertently entering the rather untidy rear of a factory, manufacturing and storing I know not what. I was not even aware that I was trespassing until I came to the much tidier and modern front of the building which sported a chain-link fence, a modern security building, and a large uniformed security guard. Luckily, like the guns at Singapore before the Japanese invasion from the land, he was facing in the direction where visitors might have been expected to come from, and didn't notice me. I decided that discretion was the better part of valour, beat a retreat the way I had come in, and followed another stretch of line.

I wended my way further, and passed the locomotive shed, which was neat and reasonably modern, and adjacent to which was a weed-killing wagon. Its maker's plate told that it had been constructed by Chas Roberts & Co of Wakefield, but had no date, which was a pity, because the thing looked rather ancient, with wooden sole bars and split-spoked wheels. "Slough Estates Ltd No 1" was painted on one side of the tank. My meanderings ceased at the weighbridge where the lines from various parts of the Estate converged, and fanned out again into sorting sidings adjacent to the Western Region mainline. No 3 arrived, bell clanging vigorously, towing the fruits of her labours, and shunted the wagons ready for collection by British Railways.

Mention of my inadvertent trespass in the Trading Estate reminds me that people like me tended to indulge from time to time in a little intentional trespassing in the name of

observing interesting railway things, or in an endeavour to secure decent photographs. One day in the late summer of 1961 I passed the goods yard at Maidenhead, where the engine of a pick-up goods was doing a little gentle sorting of wagons. The gates to the yard being open, I gently eased in, and secured a couple of pictures. Suddenly, from out of the blue, as it were, a railway policeman appeared, accompanied by a plain clothes colleague, and I was whisked into a neighbouring office. I quickly admitted to my trespass, which I tried to mitigate on the grounds that I had applied to the authorities for a line-side photographic permit, but this was to no avail. I was questioned closely and penetratingly for some long minutes. It seemed that there had been a spate of thefts from wagons and the goods shed, and the implication was clearly that I was finding out information which would enable this spate to continue. After what seemed an interminable time, I managed to persuade the gentlemen of railway law of my innocence, and I was allowed my freedom, with the admonishment that I must never trespass again. I left the office and got the hell out of the goods yard, suffering the grins of the locomotive crew and the guard as I did so. I have to confess, though, that this episode did not entirely stop my future gentle trespassing, although I was much more circumspect about how I went about it.....

I headed off in other directions, too, and on one memorable day took advantage of an old Swindon Works custom, which was the throwing open of its doors at 2.00pm for about a couple of hours on a Wednesday afternoon so that interested visitors, principally, it must be said, mainly loco-spotting boys, could see what was going on. So it came to pass that on 31 August 1960 I took a Weston-super-Mare express from Reading, and headed west. I noted that the stations to Didcot tended to look smart and business-like, but that those between Didcot and Swindon looked distinctly run-down. I was slightly frustrated because,

Rapidly approaching decay. The view north from Staines West station on 16 July 1960. Passenger services here lingered on until 29 March 1965 and were latterly served by a single unit diesel railcar.

although I kept my eyes well and truly peeled as we rattled through Wantage Road, where the Wantage Tramway had once connected with the Great Western, I failed to spot the little tank engine "Shannon" which the Great Western had saved when the tramway closed in 1945, and which they had subsequently refurbished and put on exhibition at the station.

On arrival at Swindon I killed time by visiting Swindon Old Town Station, until grouping the tangible evidence of the little Midland and South Western Junction Railway's temerity in making an intrusion into the hallowed ground of the Great Western's railway town. The place, as might be expected of a secondary route reaching the end of its days, was quiet, although a 9400 0-6-0PT was indulging in some unhurried shunting. I was always of the impression that, although the GWR acquired the M&SWJR at grouping, it did not much care for the line, and suffered its presence out of necessity rather than love.

Just before two o'clock I joined the mayhem of the party visiting Swindon Works. As already suggested much of the swarm was made up of boys, mostly clutching notebooks or Ian Allan ABC's. The horde flooded towards the erecting shop as the gates opened, and most work ceased in the face of their advance. The hair of anyone in the health and safety industry today would stand on end at the very thought of

this event, but the reality of the time was that there seemed few potential problems. The vast majority of the swarm acted responsibly and obeyed instructions. The very few who didn't were herded back into the mainstream with no difficulty. One of the things that tickled me was that the really committed spotters copied down their numbers from any part of a locomotive which had any identification on its. Thus, such relatively small items such as spring hangers or eccentric cranks with numbers chalked on them apparently counted as a "cop"! I, together with a number of more mature visitors, stayed in the more peaceful rear of the party, where we were able to have the odd conversation with railwaymen.

Outside the eastern end of the erecting shop were some sparkling examples of locomotives, both steam and diesel, in a state of newly out-shopped perfection. This seemed to me to show that there was still a deal of pride around amongst those who worked on them, and they were displayed like showpieces in an informal kind of exhibition. Inside the works the types under construction were principally B-B "Warships", but there were a few 0-6-0 204bhp diesel mechanical shunters in various stages of completion. A variety of types were undergoing overhaul, with no apparent segregation – steam and diesel seemed to be mixed indiscriminately. These weekly visits must have been disastrous for some aspects of works productivity, and

I noted one or two younger members of staff – probably apprentices – taking the opportunity for a little skive away from normal duties. One was comfortably ensconced in the bunker of a 9400 class locomotive consuming an ice lolly, and continued to do so long after the last of the swarm had passed.

I pleaded unsuccessfully with one of those shepherding the horde for a quick look at the scrap lines, which were invisible from the part of the works around which the swarm swirled, because two or three "Dukedogs" and some 0-4-0 tanks withdrawn from South Wales must have been there, but my quiet begging was to no avail. Some withdrawn derelicts were, however, visible closer at hand. The Great Western's 1950 Swiss-built Brown-Boveri gas turbine no. 18000 was there, rusty and forlorn, awaiting the breaker's torch. Amongst others were 9400 class 0-6-0PT's nos. 8448 and 8450, both withdrawn a year earlier. 8448's sister,

8447, held the unenviable record of being the shortest-lived, at four years and nine months, of all steam locomotives built by British Railways. 8448 could not have been far behind.

I returned to Swindon station, and spent time immersed in the busy railway scene. Yes, the diesel was increasing in numbers and a lot more was changing, but upon reflection this trip was probably the last time that I was truly immersed in the remains of the old Great Western steam regime.

Thereafter, my trips around Western territory were closer to home, but continued to provide interest, and constant evidence of changing times. At the end of 1961 I migrated to East Anglia, an area where the times had already largely changed, and the steam locomotive and many branch lines and traditional railway things were largely a memory.

'Kerosene Castle' to give it its unofficial name, aka gas turbine No 18000 at Swindon on 10 June 1952. Finally introduced into service in 1950 two years later than intended, this was the first of two gas turbine machines that would operate on the Western Region in the 1950s. No 18000 survived on paper at least until 1960 although as time passed and it became clear this type of technology was not to be replicated so the impetus to effect necessary repairs lessened and long periods were destined to be spent out of use at Swindon. (No 18100 had an even shorter working life.) The pointed finial was part of an adornment on the platform and not a roofline embellishment!
(John Johnstone)

Old before their time at Swindon. Redundant 'modern' pannier tanks from the 84xx and 94xx series as well as Collett 2251 0-6-0s. All laid aside on the simple basis there was just no more work for them. (NB collection)

NBL Type 1 No D6356 travelling on the down slow line near Twyford with what appears to be an unfitted freight although possibly having a 'fitted-head'.
10 February 1969.
(J H Cooper-Smith)

4

My life was then sadly Great Western free, save for books and magazine articles, for nearly a couple of years until I made visits to the West Country in August and September 1963. The first was to West Somerset with a companion who was rather unfocused on railways, and my trips and researches were thus somewhat curtailed. I did, however, get some time in at Watchet harbour, which was still a busy and thriving port rather than the haunt of yachties that it is now since it became transmuted into a marina. The busyness in those days still embraced railway goods traffic, although it wasn't to be long before the strategic thinkers of British railways lost interest, and the roads of West Somerset and the communities they passed through suffered accordingly. The imports through the docks at that time included large quantities of esparto grass, much of which was distributed by rail to various paper mills in the district, including, I think that I am right in saying, the local one on the south western outskirts of the town - a very short haul indeed, and the kind that was becoming increasingly unpopular with those who ran the railway. When I visited a Hymek diesel hydraulic was whiling away time doing nothing in particular in the goods yard at the station, and a three car diesel multiple unit towing an ordinary Mark 1 coach arrived from Taunton, paused a little, and then headed off to Minehead.

My next visit to the west was of longer duration, and three weeks after the minor entertainment in West Somerset I travelled to Torquay. At this time all west of England trains left from Platform One at Paddington, as they had for many, many years, and I was delighted that the "Cornish Riviera", which I was catching, was still obeying the tradition. That day it was headed by immaculate maroon-liveried "Western" D1057 "Western Chieftain", barely five months old and an impressive sight to behold. After a day or two I headed north from my Torquay base to participate in the clamour which was leading up to the last rights of the Culm Valley Light Railway, from Tiverton Junction to Hemyock, and the Exe Valley line. I was delighted with the Culm valley, so frequently referred to and illustrated in magazines, with its sharp curves and mixed trains that positively dawdled, particularly in the Hemyock direction, over the seven and a half mile branch. One of the many claims to fame of the Culm Valley was that it had played host to the very last two gas-lit coaches on British Railways. These were ex-Barry Railway vehicles which arrived on the line in

Nearly new 'Western' class diesel-hydraulic C-C No D1057 'Western Chieftan' is ready to depart from Platform 1 at Paddington to bear me off to Devon on the 'Cornish Riviera Express'. 5 September 1963.

43

14xx class 0-4-2T No 1471 and North British diesel-hydraulic B-B No D6318 on shed at Exeter St Davids. 7 September 1963.

the early 1950's, and were built with electric lighting. This was removed at Swindon before the transfer and replaced by gas lighting, because the aforementioned dawdle up the Culm Valley was too slow for axle-driven generators to keep the batteries charged. These were replaced by two electrically lit ex-LNER brake seconds during the winter of 1962-63 (recharging of their batteries took place by plugging them in overnight at Tiverton Junction – I wonder why no one thought of that before?), and so unfortunately I wasn't able experience gas, but I still enjoyed watching the overhang of the carriage ends as we rounded some of the sharper bends. Because of the anticipated – and actual – above normal traffic, both the coaches were in use.

I couldn't do the full length of the Exe Valley, so after leaving the Culm Valley took the "Tivvie Bumper" push-pull train on little and ancient branch from Tiverton Junction to Tiverton and travelled south from there. In spite of the impending closure of the line, diesel units were sharing brisk passenger traffic with the long-standing 1400 0-4-2T or 0-6-0PT hauled passenger trains.

In terms of the Great Western[3], for the remainder of my visit to South Devon I travelled the Kingswear branch, became acquainted with the spectacular mainline along by the Exe estuary, the coast between Dawlish Warren and Teignmouth, and the Teign estuary and spent time at a busy

Newton Abbot, not substantially changed, I fancy, since my grandfather's wartime rattyness, except that now cigarettes *were* available in the refreshment rooms. The last "proper" broad gauge engine, the vertical boilered "Tiny", late of the South Devon Railway, was still preserved on the down platform. I say "proper" because she is the only true locomotive survivor of the broad gauge, the only other possible contender being the 1837 "North Star", which is ruled out because the original was scrapped in 1906, and the 1923 version was merely a replica which incorporated some remaining components of the original. Whilst I was gazing at "Tiny" a railwayman came and stood beside me. "She'd still work today, you know" he said quietly to almost no-one in particular. "You'd only have to put a fire inside her, and off she'd go." And then he wandered quietly away. "Tiny" was eventually removed, and may now be seen in the museum of the South Devon Railway at Buckfastleigh.

During my brief stay in Devon I must have been sprinkled with a little pixie dust, because I returned to East Anglia with the certain knowledge that sooner rather than later I would become a West Country resident. The pixies were not wrong. I moved to Teignmouth in early 1964.

3. I did cover a lot of Southern ground on this visit, too, as described in "Memories of Southern Railways".

No 1450 on an auto service waiting departure from St Davids for Dulverton over the Exe Valley route.

The same train leaving and passing Red Cow Crossing hard by Exeter Middle signal box. On the left the two SR 'W' class tanks and the WR 'Pannier' are waiting their turn ready to bank trains from Exeter St Davids to Exeter Central. 7 September 1963.

14xx 0-4-2T No 1421 collecting milk tank wagons at Hemyock ready to attach these to a train for Tiverton Junction. 7 September 1963.

Above - *Penzance bound near Liskeard: the stumps of the original timber structure visible through the arch. The signal is the*
for the trains on the lower level line at Moorswater.
Below - *The terminus at Looe on he branch from Liskeard. (Both Denis Calender)*

Opposite ends of the spectrum at Old Oak Common. **Above** *- Breakdown train workshop van No W130.*
Below *- 'Super Saloon' No 9115 'Duke of Gloucester' inside the carriage shed at Old Oak Common. Out of nine of the type originally built, regrettably this was one of three destined to be scrapped. (Both Denis Calender)*

Opposite page *- Probably brand new, 0-6-0PT No 1505 outside Swindon shed. After running in this engine spent its entire working life based at old Oak Common and was disposed of when not even 13 years old. (NB collection)*

No 6841 'Marlas Grange' running into Paddington past Paddington goods depot with a stopping service formed of BR Mk1 stock. (NB collection)

Steam's Indian summer. 'Castle' No 4079 'Pendennis Castle' backing down to Paddington ready for the Ian Allan high-speed run of 9 May 1964. Both engine and tender are immaculate - the latter the second tender prepared as the first sprung a number of leaks once all the grime had been cleaned off! Sadly the attempt to replicate the 100mph run of 'City of Truro' would end in failure although not through an fault in the preparation of the engine. (NB collection)

A sight to gladden the heart of any steam man at Bristol Temple Meads. County class 4-6-0 No 1010 'County of Caernarvon' coming to the rescue of 'Warship' No D814 'Dragon', the latter having failed on a Paddington to Weston-super-Mare service, 27 August 1961. (NB collection)

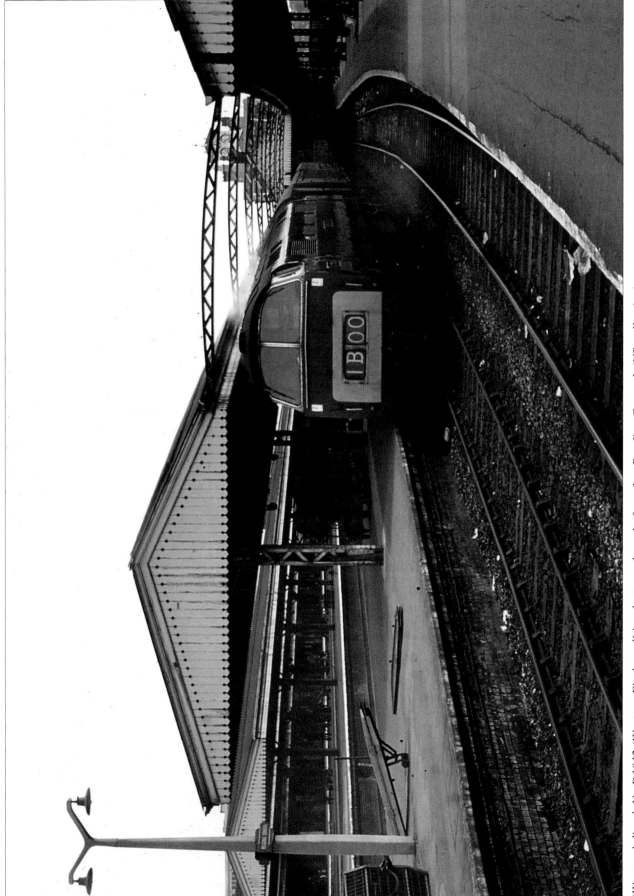

'Western' diesel, No D1012 'Western Firebrand' in what was then platform 3 at Reading General. (NB collection)

Not long for this world. No 1007 'County of Brecknock' seen at its final shed, Didcot, shortly before withdrawal. (NB collection)

61xx No 6139, which from its lack of headcode is engaged in carriage shunting at Didcot. (NB collection)

INTERLUDE 2 - DEVON BRANCH LINES

Culmstock on 24 September 1960. No 1420 complete with its train, a solitary gas-lit vehicle No W261W. (Mark B Warburton, courtesy Mrs Margaret Warburton)

Great Westernery at Uffcolme.
(Mark B Warburton, courtesy Mrs Margaret Warburton)

Hemyock terminus, 24 September 1960. The 14xx engine waits in the platform whilst the photographer with camera and tripod seems more intent on recording the young lady rather that the contemporary railway scene. 24 September 1960. (Mark B Warburton, courtesy Mrs Margaret Warburton)

No 1462 at Hemyock with milk tanks and gas-lit coach, 19 May 1959.
(Mark B Warburton, courtesy Mrs Margaret Warburton)

61

Thorverton station on the Exe Valley line from Stoke Canon to Tiverton and eventually Dulverton, captured on 9 September 1962. The long siding curving off to the right served a mill on the River Exe. *(Mark B Warburton, courtesy Mrs Margaret Warburton)*

In steam days Exeter played host to a number of 14xx 04-2T tank engines. Two examples are seen, Nos 1442 and 1451 both of which once carried green livery under their now grimy exterior. 9 September 1963
(Mark B Warburton, courtesy Mrs Margaret Warburton)

5

It was an interesting time to become an inhabitant of Great Western territory. This was a period of great change. Yes, there was the sad departure of branch line after branch line, and, yes, my beloved steam locomotives were disappearing rapidly, but in spite of all this, and, the hovering presence of Dr Beeching and some of the more dire things in his report, there was still quite a lot of positive stuff around as well. Main line passenger traffic was still heavy, there was still plenty of freight, the Western was becoming well-equipped with its own brands of diesel locomotives which were still coming off the production lines, and the late Gerard Fiennes, one of the most successful railway managers of the nationalised era – and one of the most outspoken[4] – had been appointed as Chairman of the Western Region Board and General Manager of the Western Region. There was also still more than a hint of the presence of older things and traditional ways. Echoes and shadows of the Great Western abounded, and there were a great number of reminders of things past,

sometimes long past, and I savoured with relish the notion of getting to know and experience them. So from the point of view of a railway amateur, a lot of things looked rather rosy.

I had secured a job in South Devon before my move, but it flattered to deceive, and before long I knew that I would have to seek pastures new. As a first step, I thought yet again about the possibility of working on the railway. I say "yet again" because I had made several attempts to get railway work before I left school in the late 1950's. Sadly, these attempts had produced nothing, but in the light of the fact that I now had nearly five years of pen-pushing experience to offer as well as my rather unexciting educational qualifications, I travelled to BR's Divisional Headquarters in Plymouth to see what was around. Unfortunately, I soon learned that there was not a lot around, and vaunt my pen-pushing expertise as I might, the only vacancy for which any of my expertise and experience came close to being suitable was that of booking clerk at Exeter Central. It was made quite clear to me in my interview that this was a job involving shift work. I really didn't mind about the shift work, but when I asked about the

4. Gerard Fiennes, a life-long railwayman, had his autobiography "I Tried to Run a Railway" published in 1967 by Ian Allan. As a result of his comments in the book about the way in which he felt the railways were being managed, he was carpeted by the Board, and subsequently left the employ of the railway.

Devoid of its BR smokebox numberplate, 14xx 0-4-2T No 1421 pauses at Uffcombe with a train for Hemyock. 7 September 1963.

The Tiverton Junction-Tiverton push-pull train - the "Tivvy Bumper" - headed by 14xx class 0-4-2T No. 1466, waits for passengers at Tiverton Junction. 7 September 1963.

and during the day on Saturdays in the holiday season from other parts of the United Kingdom to a variety of destinations in Devon and Cornwall. Although this kind of traffic was a little diminished from the halcyon days of the 1950's, there were still plenty of travellers, and on many early Saturday trips I had to make in the summer the coaches of the trains were full of dishevelled, bleary-eyed travellers who had started their journeys in the Midlands in the small hours, or in the north even earlier. It was usually easier to stand in a corridor than to try to secure a seat amongst piles of luggage and sprawled bodies.

For four or five years I spent many hours pursuing railway things, and became very familiar with the Great Western mainline, particularly in South Devon. Western steam was all but non-existent in the area, even when I arrived in Devon, but there were occasional sightings to be had, and for the first few months of my tenure there were signs of steam activity. I lived close to the station at Teignmouth, and the usual audible sounds were the rattling whine of the engines of diesel hydraulics, but every now and then, usually when I was frustratingly unable to see anything, there was the sound of a steam whistle. In my early commuting days there were a couple of occasions when the train was steam-hauled.

As might be expected in the dying days of steam, we had a number of last runs. The Railway Correspondence and Travel Society and Plymouth Railway Circle organised the "Cornubian", a final steam-hauled trip from Exeter to Penzance on 3rd May 1964. Six days later came Ian Allan's "Castle" hauled final run from Paddington to Plymouth, giving a last opportunity to see brass safety valve covers and copper-capped chimneys.

Aside from ex-Southern locations in the area steam was still extant in the shape of banking engines at Exeter St Davids, and we had at least one visit at St Davids from a clean 4700 2-8-0 which brought in a block cement train from Westbury, the Presflo wagons destined for the now long-closed Blue Circle Portland Cement depot at Exeter Central. On another day the bulk cement train, which was a regular working, was noisily taken up the hill to Central by four tank engines – two heading the train, and two banking at the rear. North from Exeter, until the line between Tiverton Junction and Tiverton was closed in October 1964 the motive power for the "Tivvy Bumper" push-pull train was a 1400 class 0-4-2T, and the old order still hung on at Taunton, just, whilst the dying branches from there to Barnstaple, Minehead and Yeovil still used at least some steam.

The final steam special train of that era, organised again by the RCTS and the PRC, was the "Exmoor Ranger", which

times of shifts, I had no option but to demur. "Early's" meant being on duty at 5.30 a.m., and as the first train in the morning from Teignmouth arrived in Exeter at a few minutes past seven, that was clearly not on. In those days I didn't drive, either. When I mentioned these facts of life to my interviewer, he didn't seem all that worried about the possibility of losing my talent and enthusiasm, and rather implied that they were my problem. Once again, the railway failed to secure my services, such as they were, and I had to search elsewhere to make a living.

Instead of the excitement of being a railway employee, I secured a reasonably unexciting and reasonably unrewarded job in neighbouring Newton Abbot, to which I could commute by train. Unexciting it may have been, but nevertheless, it was a job, and amongst other changes in my life for the first time in four years I found myself having to work on Saturday mornings. One of the long-standing traditions of the "Great Way West" was the relatively huge number of through trains which ran overnight on Fridays

Opposite bottom - The bridge carrying Barn Park Road over Teignmouth railway station was renewed in April-May 1965. During renewal it was revealed that the support for the highway was provided by broad gauge Barlow rails. This photograph shows the rails being removed. Today's health and safety people wouldn't be too pleased. 24 April 1965.

Top - *The last real broad gauge locomotive. South Devon Railway 0-4-0VB "Tiny" preserved on the down platform at Newton Abbot. "She'd still work today....you'd only have to put a fire inside her, and off she'd go." 9 September 1963. (See p44).*

1964, and the broad gauge still lives on - a bit. Remnants of broad gauge on a quay at Sutton Harbour, Plymouth. 13 September 1964.

toured the remains of the North Devon lines from Exeter St Davids on 27th March 1965. The locomotive for the Ilfracombe, Barnstaple, Taunton and Exeter leg was 2251 class 0-6-0 3205. It was rumoured that this was the last locomotive to use the turntable at Taunton motive power depot, which was closed for ever after the engine had departed.

In terms of regular trains, a pretty busy summer Saturday service was maintained, with passenger trains still connecting Devon and Cornwall with many places in the rest of the United Kingdom. Overcrowding was still common on many workings, and seat regulation tickets were much used. For those unfamiliar with the seat regulation system, it was simply a device which tried to ensure that the number travel tickets issued for any one train did not exceed the number of seats available. I am not sure that it always worked completely, because, as far as I can remember, there was no allocation of actual seats, and I can remember that on some occasions when I travelled, it was more comfortable to stand in the corridor or end vestibule of carriages rather than to fight one's way into an already pretty full compartment. Admittedly, my journeys were only of fairly short duration. Had I been travelling the full length of the journey I might have taken my chances with the fight.

In remembrance, there was still an essence of Great Western holiday magic around the sunny summer Saturdays which we enjoyed, recollection suggests, rather a lot of in those days. This was enhanced by the fact that in spite of most coaches being in the standard, since 1956, maroon livery, there were still a lot of chocolate and cream liveried specimens around, and that the majority of the locomotives were still Brunswick green, not at all unlike the old steam

locomotive colour, even if the Brunswick green was sometimes supplemented by other shades. Actually, the Brunswick green engines and maroon carriages were not a bad colour combination, but one of the better schemes was created by the maroon coloured "Westerns" with maroon coaches. There had been experiments with liveries with this class. The first one was out-shopped with a livery described as "desert sand", the second was coloured maroon, and then a few more early examples were released in Brunswick green garb, before maroon was used again. British Railways then actually asked the public which they preferred, and maroon was the final choice. The exception to this rule was D1015 which emerged in something called "golden ochre". After 1966, all liveries were swept away in the face of the new corporate livery of "rail blue", a colour which suited some coaching stock quite well, but which in my opinion, never looked really right on locomotives.

During the first year after my move to Devon, my state of mind also moved. Perhaps my two years in a completely non-steam and diminished branch line network East Anglia might have been an influence, but I gradually decided that there was little point in continuing to mourn in depth the unalterable demise of the steam locomotive, and to be merely regretful of the, apparently sometimes stupid, decisions about line closures and the letting go of certain sorts of traffic. I began to rather welcome the fact that, although a number of things were not as they once were, at least we still had a busy train service, usually hauled by largely new locomotives, and, at the time our pretty progressive management was overseeing technical developments such as the installation of all-electric signalling in the Plymouth area, and, using the modern locomotives and rolling stock, initiating useful changes to train services. A great example of the latter was the introduction in 1964 of the fastest-ever train, at that time, between Plymouth and Paddington, the "Golden Hind", with six especially maintained "Western" diesels (the "Golden stud"), all reserved seats, and hand-picked restaurant car crews, which very quickly became so popular a service to the extent that it was often full to capacity with potential travellers being turned away.

So although things may not have been utterly perfect, there was still a lot of rosiness to appreciate, and a lot of vigour to celebrate, in spite of Dr Beeching's best efforts and the existence of various governmental and other nay-sayers. We had successfully coped with the days of Ernest Marples and the late and un-lamented Railway Conversion League, which had campaigned in the late fifties and the early sixties for the conversion of the entire railway network into a system of highways[5]. There seemed to be a lot that was potentially worthwhile to look forward to.

5. The curious thinking of the rail to road campaigners largely disappeared altogether by the 1970's, but still occasionally rears its head in the current century.

In spite of my perhaps slightly grudging acceptance of the developing *status quo* I was also very comfortable with the presence of the great number of indications of history which was around in those days. Aside from older locomotives and rolling stock there were numerous items which originated in earlier times, and which were still in daily use. Take for example the great number of Great Western lower quadrant semaphore signals which abounded, and of which there are still examples extant at the time of writing, or the platform seats with "GWR" supports, numbers of which are still around, and, of course, cast notices with directions and warnings (I should have paid closer attention to the "Trespassing on the Railway" variety earlier in the pursuit of my passion for railways, as already recounted!).

One of the delights of a West Country sojourn was the fact that everywhere there was evidence of former railways and the industries they had served in many places. My pre-residential West Country visit to Somerset in 1963 had yielded a wagon turntable with ex-broad gauge bridge rails at Watchet harbour, and had given me my first acquaintance with the remains of the fascinating West Somerset Mineral Railway, built in the late 1850's to transport iron ore from the Brendon Hills to Watchet for shipment to South Wales. After initial success the traffic declined and the railway underwent a number of incarnations until the track was lifted in 1917, and the remaining assets sold off in 1924, but

when I was introduced to its remains the tremendous earthworks of the incline down which loaded wagons of ore were lowered from Brendon Hill were still a great landmark, as they still are today.

There were signs that, in a way, the broad gauge was still with us. In August 1965 there was some tangible evidence of track-work still embedded in the quay at Sutton Harbour in Plymouth, and other lengths of bridge rail were disinterred later from Teignmouth Docks. I had long been aware of great amounts of redundant bridge rail used as fence posts and notice board supports all around the Great Western system. I was bold enough to mention this in an article in the "Railway Magazine", and was subsequently chastised by the late C R Clinker who claimed that all the posts were actually the result of separate orders from Swindon, and were nothing to do with bridge rail. Although much of me felt that I shouldn't have the audacity to challenge an acknowledged expert in railway matters, I felt that I couldn't buy this, and a brief correspondence ensued! Close to home, a road bridge over the cutting in which the east end of Teignmouth Station nestled was replaced in April and May 1965, and as demolition of the existing structure progressed an exciting find was revealed. The whole supporting floor of the roadway was made from discarded Barlow rails. I think that this caused some excitement amongst the railway fraternity, and a couple of lengths were despatched from the long-gone down goods

4' 6" gauge Lee Moor Peckett 0 -4-0ST No 2 undergoing preservation work. Primed, but not painted. 5 June 1966

yard, to the National Railway Museum collection, so I was told.

There was some excitement to be found, too, on the beach at Goodrington, south of Paignton on the Kingswear branch, too. Undisturbed for many, many years, and unnoticed by the vast majority of residents and holidaymakers who passed them by daily, were the pipes used to drain the land adjacent to the railway. Their fame and interest lay in the fact that they were made up of the pipes used in the South Devon Railway's early life as an atmospheric line. Aside from these, the demise of the atmospheric had left little behind it, but the pumping house at Starcross remained, and remains, together with the remnants of the never-used pumping houses at Torre and Totnes.

I made a succession of exploratory visits to what was left of a range of historic railways, of which we had an abundance in Devon and Cornwall.

Early on was a visit to the remains of the Liskeard and Caradon with its route to the derelict, but once incredibly busy, mining district around Caradon and the granite quarries at Cheesewring, and at Kilmar Tor further on into the wild wastes of Bodmin Moor. For those whose knowledge of this early and perhaps slightly peculiar railway is limited, it was opened in 1846 to connect the mines and quarries with the Looe Canal (fore-runner of the later Looe branch which replaced it in 1879) at Moorswater near Liskeard. The history of the railway is fascinating, and its fortunes were inevitably linked to the fortunes of the mines and quarries, varying between good profits and penury. The way in which the line was constructed and worked in its early days did not come up to Board of Trade requirements, and thus precluded its use by fare-paying passengers. For a time the company got around this awkward bureaucratic stuff by issuing passengers with free passes, and charging them for items that they had with them, such as hats and parcels. More orthodox railway practice became the norm after the steeply graded and sharply curved connection between Liskeard station and Moorswater was opened in 1901, and the Great Western took over working the Liskeard and Caradon and Liskeard and Looe lines in 1909. The Moorswater to Caradon portion was closed on 1 January 1917, although much of the track was lifted before that date and shipped to Europe for help with the war effort. When I visited the remains in 1965, however, there was much to see, including stone blocks which had supported the original rails, and track that was still unlifted in Cheesewring Quarry. This might have thwarted some of the war effort!

Another interesting excursion was to the unique Haytor Granite Tramway on the eastern side of Dartmoor, which in traditional terms *was* a proper tramway, being laid with lengths of granite fashioned in the manner of a plateway.[6] The relics of this interesting transport oddity were, and still are, a tribute to pre- Victorian engineering ingenuity. The line was very early in the history of Devon railways, predating the Plymouth and Dartmoor, so there were no great local examples of railways or plateways to stimulate its design. In the their absence what could be more practical, then, that to use the plentiful supply of local materials to construct a transport link to connect the Haytor Quarries with the Stover Canal, close to Newton Abbot, to enable granite to be shipped by barge to Teignmouth, and onwards to its final destination by sea? Haytor granite was used in a number of important contracts, including London Bridge and parts of the British Museum. The tramway was opened in 1820, but was disused by 1858, and its route south of Bovey Tracey was used for the construction of part of the Moretonhampstead and South Devon Railway. The extensive remains of the tramway between Bovey Tracey and Haytor will probably last for centuries.

The other side of Dartmoor yielded the last surviving, but disused example, of the 4' 6" ("Dartmoor") gauge in the shape of the Lee Moor Tramway, a cousin, as it were, of the previously-mentioned and long-gone Plymouth and Dartmoor Railway. The Lee Moor's two little Peckett 0-4-0 saddle tanks survived at the top end of the line, and at this time one of them – No. 2 – was in the early throes of preservation. Both locomotives were eventually saved; No 1 rests at the Wheal Martin China Clay Museum in Cornwall, and No 2 has found its way to the South Devon Railway at Buckfastleigh, where it has joined "Tiny", after a period of exhibition at the National Trust's Saltram House at Plympton.

Further west, the remains of the Hayle Railway's Portreath branch and the earlier Portreath Tramway, various china clay backwaters and remnants of Treffrys tramway came in for my attention. I traced the route, too, of the little narrow gauge Pentewan Railway, and did the same with the rather wider gauged Redruth and Chasewater. There were few signs left of the 2'6" gauge Pentewan, although it was pleasing to find that when I visited there were still some rails used to move sand around at the harbour. I was assured though that these were not relics of the original line, and that the use of the same gauge was purely coincidental. The Redruth and Chasewater was clearly traceable, and there was a range of tangible remains, which was quite a surprise, considering that this independent and physically

6. Or, maybe, not quite unique. There was another tramway made of stone built around 1750 at Conisborough, near Doncaster.

Opposite page, top - *View looking down the remains of the West Somerset Mineral Railway's tremendous incline at Brendon Hill. 14 August 1963.*

Opposite page, bottom - *The WSMR's winding house at the top of the Brendon Hill incline, viewed from the east. 14 August 1963.*

isolated 4'0" gauge line had disappeared well over fifty years before my visit.

Back to modern times, I paid countless visits to various parts of the Western network, largely in South Devon, and there was always plenty of activity to be photographed from traditional and new locations. Modern stuff notwithstanding, on a trip to London I was pleased to be able to record the last regular steam working from Paddington, the 16.15 to Bicester, drawn on the occasion of my visit by No. 7915 "Mere Hall". I know that it was the end of an era, but my new-found sanguinity saw me take it as all part of the progress of things.

Towards the end of 1965, I visited Bristol Bath Road diesel depot, which was adjacent to Bristol Temple Meads Station. It was a redevelopment of the important steam depot which closed in 1960, and, although one of the turntables from steam days was retained, its design and facilities were largely state of the art. Like so many things from those days, state of the art or not, it has long since ceased to exist, being closed in September 1995, with demolition reducing it

to an extended heap of rubble before the site was given over to light industrial usage. The area is now known as the "Temple Quarter Enterprise Zone", scarcely, in my view, an exciting title. As could be said over many once important railway locations "Ichabod, for the glory is departed."

On the occasion of my visit, the place was busy enough with a variety of diesel types, but one of the most striking things was the number of Class 14 0-6-0 diesel hydraulics, ordered from Swindon in early 1963, and delivered from 1964 onwards, that were already giving the impression of their later reputation as white elephants. This was a pity. Of their kind they were quite handsome machines, but by the time that they appeared, the implementation of some of the recommendations of the Beeching report meant that their *raisons d'etre* – shunting, trip-work and short distance freight – were rapidly ceasing to exist, hence a line of them lying out of commission at Bath Road. And most were but a year and a bit at the most or just a few months old at the least. With the benefit of hindsight one might well ask "How was that for a sensible piece of capital expenditure.....?" and "Wouldn't it have been better to keep a fleet of pannier tanks operating instead until the results of the new order became obvious?" The Class 14's present, incidentally, included No. D9555 of 1965, the last locomotive to be built at Swindon. A few years earlier, whoever would have thought it possible that Swindon would have been written off? It is only fair to record that the vast majority of the class were sold, doubtless for a favourable price, to industries that used rail transport for their own internal use, but were gradually made redundant again as the industries, principally coal and steel, which had become adoptive parents, themselves declined. A number subsequently became the property of the preservation movement and are still around, and a couple, with appropriate alterations, even made it to Spain for a further lease of life in industrial use.

Top - 4575 class 2-6-2T No 5555 'dead' at Exeter St Davids MPD. The missing numberplates and cover over the chimney does not bode well for a return to use. 7 September 1963. (the engine was in fact officially withdrawn from service with effect from 31 July.)

Right - A row of white elephants. Class 14 diesel hydraulic 0-6-0's D9500, D9527, D9504, D9523, D9553 lined up at Bristol Bath Road MPD. Not dead, merely sleeping. 6 November 1965.

In 1972, almost without thinking, I embarked on one of the biggest railway associated adventures of my life. This adventure, though, had nothing to do with locomotives and journeys, and everything to do with Great Western history, and was also, so it transpired, an epic of hard work.

This was a period of inexorable house price inflation and gazumping. In spite of this, and the fact that our resources were extremely limited, my then wife was keen to indulge in house ownership, and knowing that with things as they were, it was clearly going to be well nigh impossible to climb conventionally on to the property ladder. I was aware that it was often the case in those days that large organisations, particularly public ones, sometimes didn't seem to understand the value of some of their less-used assets, and so I wrote to the British Rail Property Board enquiring if they had any disused property or land suitable for development within commuting distance of Exeter, where I then worked. After something of a wait, their reply

arrived with details of six redundant stations. Someone clearly had an interesting view of "commuting distance from Exeter", because all but one were not really in that league. There were places in the depths of East Somerset, and another on the disused Newquay to Chacewater line in Cornwall. The only possible contender was Lustleigh, on the Newton Abbot to Moretonhampstead branch, and after some soul-searching and with few funds, we put in a tender for the place. I was fairly comfortable with this, because initial enquiries at the planning office suggested that there was a great deal of interest in the place, and I rated our chances of acquisition as being low.

After six weeks there was a letter from the BR Property Board. Our tender had been accepted! I suspect that others had been put off by the existence of a restrictive covenant imposed by the owner of the land on which the station was built when it was conveyed to the railway to the effect that no dwelling place was ever to be built on it, by the fact that

Taken on the same day as the view opposite, another one that was redundant as the traffic it once handled no longer existed. 64xx No 6421 at Exeter St Davids awaiting scrap. Alongside to the right is 14xx No 1470 also having turned its last wheel in service. No 6421 had been out of service since January 1963 and was disposed of at the South Wales scrapyards in October 1963. It had existed for 28 years. No 1470 had been out of service slightly longer, officially withdrawn on 31 October 1962. It too was destined for South Wales and was slightly younger at just 26 years old.

Above and below - Lustleigh as was. The South Devon Railway Society 'Heart of Devon Rambler' tour seen at the station on 6 June 1960. 2-6-2T No 4174 was used from Paignton to Newton Abbot, Bovey Tracey and Mortonhampstead and return. At this stage goods traffic was also still being handled. *(Mark B Warburton, courtesy Mrs Margaret Warburton)*

there was a private railway-owned footpath through the land, and that there was a stated complete lack of main services. My life became an immediate flurry of activity involving banks, planners, local authorities, architects and lawyers, and in due course we became owners of a little derelict building set in an acre and a quarter of unkempt land not too far from the centre of a beautiful and popular village.

Although I knew of the place well before, half by chance almost, I acquired it, I was pretty much unaware of anything but its basic history. I had taken though possession of something of a gem. A Newton and Moretonhampstead railway had been mooted in 1858, and formally became the Moretonhampstead and South Devon Railway in 1861. Its Act of Parliament received the Royal Assent in July 1862, and it was opened throughout in July 1866. The line was subsequently absorbed by the South Devon Railway in 1872, which in turn became part of the GWR in 1876. After its opening, as with all railways, it assumed a regular place in the lives of the communities that it served, but Lustleigh, being the kind of community that it was gave its station a little more depth of history than for many that became rural

idylls. This was helped along by a gentleman named Cecil Torre, who lived in the Manor in a part of the greater Lustleigh community called Wreyland, which is about half a mile from the railway station. Torre, his father and grandfather were referred to as "the squire" by local people, but this seems to have been an unofficial kind of title. Cecil Torre published a collection of items from his own, his father's and his grandfather's diaries in three volumes entitled "Small Talk At Wreyland", published in 1923. This collection contains some delightful references to the life of the village, but from my point of view a greater delight is the inclusion of a number of observations relating to the railway in general, and to Lustleigh station in particular. There are graphic reports of the behaviour of the navvies building the line, and of the need to involve the militia to curb their antics. Another anecdote from late broad gauge times is about a certain engine driver on the evening train who would use the locomotive's whistle to give displays of hooting, and who would stay on over time whistling if the owls were answering back. Torre also had some interesting things to say about the reduction in share values that the original owners suffered as their assets were acquired by the SDR and then the GWR.

Lustleigh as it became, rebuilding in 1974/75. When complete the former booking office was a lot more comfortable than had been in the time of Mr Hayward........(see page 82).

Glorious Devon and the foothills of Dartmoor. No 4174 with the Heart of England Rambler special Moretonhampstead. (Mark B Warburton, courtesy Mrs Margaret Warburton)

As well as its long-standing indigenous population, Lustleigh has long attracted people of repute of some sort. Recently we have had rock musicians, merchant bankers and the odd captain of industry or two. In former times the village was home, amongst others, to sometimes quite high ranking retired military officers, a famous mountaineer and others of an artistic bent, including, it is said, the jazz violinist Stéphane Grappelli[7] who had connections there for a while. The station staff at Lustleigh knew their regulars, famous or otherwise, and their habits well. There are stories of individuals being helped in the direction of their homes after a little over-indulgence in hostelries in the towns from which they travelled, or in the restaurant cars of the trains which brought them to Newton Abbot. For some years between the wars, the Station Master kept a visitors' book to record those of note who used the station.

So it turned out that we had come by a place of more than usual interest, which was a great pleasure.

Just to tie up the pretty well known history of Lustleigh Station and the Moretonhampstead branch, here is a brief sketch of the remainder of its railway life. The broad gauge became standard gauge in 1892. Thereafter, through years of prosperity and gentle decline, the branch line and Lustleigh station quietly served their populations until passenger services were withdrawn in February 1959. The section between Bovey and Moretonhampstead, which included Lustleigh was closed completely in 1964, and the track was lifted the following year. After that, the station, boarded up, stood solidly whilst its surroundings became more and more overgrown, much to the chagrin of various individuals and bodies. Various schemes for building and the site's re-use were suggested and rejected, and then I came along, and our adventure began.

Not long after we became the lucky owners, a friend of mine

in Teignmouth introduced me to a retired Great Western railwayman who had worked on the Moretonhampstead branch. It was a lucky crossing of paths, and we had a very jolly evening talking through his reminiscences. These appear in this book as a separate section, and, I think, really give a flavour of what some aspects of rural railway life were like in the days before the Great War.

To conclude this section of my memories, I shall just say that when I took on the job of converting and extending the little structure that was Lustleigh Station, I had little or no idea of building construction. My knowledge up to that time was limited to wiring plugs and putting up shelves and applying licks of paint, and the years after the purchase were a constant round of learning and labouring for every trade. It was hard work sometimes, but the local people - mainly the working ones - were always supportive and incredibly helpful. To further support my previous comment about organisations sometimes not knowing the value of what they have, we very soon discovered that there *were* main services to the station; we had both water and drainage. All right, they needed some attention, but they *were* there! When I spoke with the BR Property Board about their existence, requiring confirmation of their uninterrupted use under neighbouring land still owned by the railway, I was called a "Lucky b----r". All notes that they were there had obviously been deleted when files were moved from place to place as various area offices opened and closed.

When we finally took up residence in the spring of 1975, although things were by no means finished, I felt great pride in what had been accomplished thus far, and through subsequent further bouts of building and extension over a number of years, finished up with a house, full of history and a pleasure to live in, in an undeniably lovely place. But all this last is another story.

Left - The outward journey of the special, seen here at Bovey Tracey. (Mark B Warburton, courtesy Mrs Margaret Warburton)

Right - In the same year as the special train seen opposite, Swindon had completed the last new steam engine to be built for British Railways, No 92220 'Evening Star'. It might have been the end of new-built but engines were still being overhauled. No 4104 freshly outshopped and with No 2834 behind. 31 August 1960.

7. Stéphane Grappelli (1908-1997) founded the Quintette du Hot Club de France with guitarist Django Reinhardt in 1934.

NOTES OF A CONVERSATION ON 27 NOVEMBER 1972 WITH MR LONG, SOMETIME MEMBER OF LUSTLEIGH STATION STAFF

I cannot, of course, vouch for the accuracy of these reminiscences, but the long conversation was like a vivid glimpse of times past which gave an added dimension to my construction and conversion efforts with Lustleigh station

I was living in Teignmouth in 1972 when I purchased Lustleigh Railway Station, intending to convert it into a dwelling. On 26th November that year I was fortunate enough to have a long conversation with a Mr Long, a retired railwayman who also lived in Teignmouth, after we had been introduced to each other by a mutual friend. I never found out Mr Long's Christian name (even in 1972 he was a man of very precise Victorian and Edwardian manners!), but he had a grand fund of memories of railway life, and we had a most entertaining evening whilst he regaled me with some of them, somewhat helped by a bottle of whisky.

Mr Long had joined the Great Western Railway as a boy of fourteen in 1912 or 1913, and worked initially at Moretonhampstead station. Once weekly – possibly on a Wednesday – his duties required him to travel to Lustleigh for a few hours to assist the station staff there. The permanent staff at Lustleigh in those days consisted of a Stationmaster and a Porter. Mr Long's brother also worked for the GWR, later spending some time at Lustleigh as Stationmaster (although I have no independent evidence of this) retiring from railway service to live at Stoke Cannon.

During the time Mr Long worked at Lustleigh, Freddie Hayward was the Stationmaster. Concurrently, Freddie Hayward's brother was Stationmaster at Bovey; it must have been a fairly rare situation for siblings to manage adjoining stations.

At that time Lustleigh had more than its fair share of retired Army Officers and maiden ladies, some of whom Mr Long described as "wealthy". Mr Long hinted that Mr Hayward might have been "a bit of a ladies' man", and he was certainly in the habit of serving one of the aforementioned maiden ladies. Mr Long's proof of this came about in an amusing way.

His first youthful appearance at Lustleigh found him wondering what sort of "lower level" duties he might have to undertake, and he was highly delighted when we was soon instructed by the Station Master to take his – the Station Master's – dog for a walk over the fields. "Make it a good long walk. He's an energetic dog and needs a lot of exercise. Take your time. I'll look after things here...." was the general gist of the instruction. The boy, hardly believing his luck, did as he was told, happy to be away from work for a while. This became a regular duty in the early part of his weekly hours at Lustleigh, and he certainly wasn't going to complain. One day, however, the "energetic dog" got away and made his way back to the Station, with the boy in hot pursuit, probably arriving back there about an hour earlier than usual. Because of this unexpected early arrival, the boy nervously sought out the Station Master to explain things, and discovered him locked in the booking office with one of the maiden ladies in a splendid state of *in flagrante delicto*.

Mr Long's many memories of Lustleigh station sixty years or so before our meeting were still clear. The shed with sliding doors adjacent to the Bovey end of the station building was for the storage of parcels and small goods items. The shed on the opposite side of the road which led to the goods yard, adjacent to the start of the footpath to the village which passed by the Cleave Hotel, was used for odd jobs, such as chopping wood. Adjacent to it was a well, and a pump located in the lamp room (next door to the gents' toilet) drew supplies of water from the well. There was another shed in the station garden opposite the Bovey end of the platform which served as a hut and store for the permanent way ganger (the remains of this were just about visible when I purchased the station). The signal-box on the platform was disused well before Mr Long's time, but he confirmed that it must have been as superfluous as Cecil Torre's father, quoted in "Small Talk At Wreyland", suspected that Lustleigh's signalling system was. Mr Long said that when he was there the signal-box was enjoying a new lease of life as a greenhouse where plants were raised for the station gardens.

The ganger who looked after the length of track from Moretonhampstead to Lustleigh used a rail-borne pedal tricycle, known as the "Velocipede" for his work. The staff at Lustleigh borrowed it on one occasion to go to a dance in Bovey, leaving it overnight at Lustleigh. Because the ganger started his day at Moretonhampstead, the "Velocipede" had to be sent there on the first train next morning.

Traffic on the railway was normally rather light, although some items, such as rabbits, were carried in quantity. The baskets used for these feature on a 1912 Chapman photograph of the station. Rabbits were shipped to markets in a number of big cities, including London, Birmingham and Sheffield.

For many years the gardens at the station were well-tended and practically immaculate. Plenty of time between trains allowed proper attention to be given to them, and they were a source of some pride to the station staff and residents of the village alike. From time-to-time some of the more well-to-do residents sent their own gardeners to the station with plants and advice to the porter who tended the station gardens.

A well-known landmark in the station garden was the grave of a much-loved station cat, which was situated opposite the signal box. The "headstone" was made of wood, faced with sheet metal, painted black with the inscription in white. The inscription on it read:

Beneath this slab, and stretched out flat,
Lies "Jumbo", once our station cat.

The former worthies of the feline race
Celestial mice o'er floor of azure chase.
Thro' meads of aromatic verdure stray –
Or purring, leap from out the Milky Way.

The second verse of the inscription has not often been reproduced. The lines were penned by one C. Hancock (was he porter at the station?). The "headstone" was topped with the initials "IHS". Some local ladies of the church complained about this, because IHS is an ancient monogram of "Jesus Christ", but Mr Hancock explained things away by saying that in the case of the cat's grave the initials stood for "I Have Suffered"! Mr Long said that Jumbo was run over by a train, although I believe that Ceil Torre suggests that he spent a lifetime jumping in and out between the wheels of trains, but died peacefully in bed. It has been written Jumbo's successor certainly met a premature end under the wheels of a train.

Although it was well after his time on the Moretonhampstead branch, Mr Long confirmed the use of Lustleigh station for the Gainsborough Pictures 1931 film of "The Hound of the Baskervilles". It became "Baskerville" for a short season, and "passengers" from the train were carried away by horse and dog-cart. It was said that Arthur Conan Doyle himself visited the station during the filming. Being a small wayside country station, there was not too much of technical note about Lustleigh. Mr Long recalled that the telegraph instrument which was located in the booking office was of the single-needle variety. The call sign for Lustleigh was "LL", and "RT" signified "End of message". The point lever for the single siding was unlocked using an Annett's Key on the train staff which was carried on locomotives to permit entry into single-line sections of the railway (Newton Abbot-Heathfield, Heathfield-Bovey and Bovey-Moretonhampstead) as required by the block system.

Sending his first-ever message on the telegraph system was a nerve-racking experience for Mr Long as a fresh young boy. During one of his normal days at Moretonhampstead potatoes were being loaded, and the stock of tarpaulins for covering the loaded wagons had run out. Lustleigh had a few in stock, and he was instructed to send a message requesting that they be put on the next train. This he did, but his nervousness caused him to omit the station code, and he was delighted and relieved when the train duly arrived with the tarpaulins on board. Mr Long described how proficient many regular users of the telegraph were. They could send continuous text with no spaces between the words, and some could tell what message was being spelled out without looking at the instrument. He considered that in many ways the old telegraph was superior to the later-installed telephone system.

Although life working for the GWR in Mr Long's young days was not very financially rewarding – to start with he received ten shillings per week, and his lodgings were nine shillings and sixpence – the unhurried atmosphere of the Moretonhampstead branch line was some compensation. The Station Master at Moretonhampstead was a real father figure, and there were breaks in routine when time was taken out for various pastimes, such as rabbiting.

Mr Long's quiet rural idyll was replaced by a much busier life when after a little while he was transferred to the post of junior at Exeter Middle signal box. This was adjacent to the level crossing at the north end of St David's station (known as Red Cow crossing) and he found himself surrounded by block instruments, telephones and 120 levers. He described himself as being a little despairing at first, thinking "I can't do this....", but of course he did do it, becoming competent enough to eventually become signalman at Churston.

After describing this move, he felt that his evening of anecdotes was drawing to an end (and the whisky bottle was nearly empty), but told me a last amusing story about his time at Exeter. As previously mentioned, the Middle box was next door to the level crossing. On one market day the crossing was closed to allow the passage of a train, and a number of farmers in carts and on horseback was waiting to cross the line. The train in question was the "Limited" (later the "Cornish Riviera"), which ran non-stop from Paddington to Plymouth. Although not time-tabled to stop, passengers for Taunton and Exeter were carried, using slip coaches which were uncoupled from the rear of the train some distance from the stations they were to serve. This meant that the main train went rapidly through the station, followed after a short while by the detached coach which coasted to a halt at its platform. On this particular market day this duly happened, as usual. The "Limited" rattled through accelerating on its way towards Plymouth, the level crossing remained closed to the farmers and others, and then the slip coach drifted by sedately. As this happened, one of the farmers rose in his cart, brandished his whip towards the slip coach and shouted up to the signal box "Yer! Tha' there train - he'm brock in 'arf!".

7

The years progressed, and I was a regular use of the old Great Western, travelling mostly on business, but still absorbed with the way the railway ran, and the places it served. Inevitably, I suppose, though, at this point in time, the memories of most interest to most people might be my older ones from the fifties, sixties and early seventies. Suffice it to say, then, that this is probably not a bad place to start to wind things down.

As the end of my narrative approaches, it would be all too easy to lapse into the mode of "things ain't what they used to be", but, perhaps reflective of my nineteen sixties optimism about what much of the Western Region seemed to be doing, I feel that this would not be completely appropriate. To be sure, there are many things that are not what they were, and which are sadly missed, but all is not sadness and woe. Over the years positive things have happened. Local authorities have lobbied heavily on behalf the railway, certainly in the west, and this has helped to retain and even enhance services. The mainline west of Plymouth has survived several propositions for its closure. New and refurbished stations have appeared all over the network, and currently there is considerable dwelling, at least as far as politicians pontification is concerned, on "updating the infrastructure" – electrification of lines from London to Bristol and South Wales, the Crossrail project and the modernisation of Reading Station to the likes of you and me. There have been a few false starts and hiccups, too. When, after privatisation, Great Western (not First Great Western) won the first franchise for express services to Wales and the West Country there was much enthusiastic talk about reinstating through coaches to Torbay and other South Devon Towns by once again dividing trains at Exeter St Davids or perhaps Newton Abbot, as in days of yore. Enthusiasm is always welcome, but I feel that the enthusiasts in this case had not really studied the nature of the High Speed Train sets, which clearly militated against such a reinstatement! A motor rail service from London to the West *was* reinstated, but sadly didn't last very long. Against heavy odds, though, the Paddington – Penzance sleeper has survived, and the last restaurant car with at seat silver service in the kingdom still gives pleasure on a couple of workings between Plymouth and Paddington every day.

Although the HST's used on the South Wales and South West express services are now over thirty years old, they have been much refurbished, and still provide the comfort afforded by a proper train, unlike some of the other newer horrors which exist elsewhere. The Cross Country "Voyager" trains, for example, have acquired the reputation of being a by-word in discomfort and travelling misery, and show the HST's to have a kind of Great Western classiness about them, which hints that the mantle has been passed on in a way, and some kind of specialness still exists. Oh, joy.

I'm sorry to limit the last words to a particular area, but, in spite of such glories as the Berkshire Downs and the beauties of Wales, for me they really must belong to the territory I chose to occupy in the early 1960's – the Devon and Cornwall peninsula. One may still ride into Exeter down part of the lovely Exe Valley, and skirt the Exe estuary with its myriad seabirds before arriving at the sea coast for the astounding scenery of the stretch from Dawlish Warren to Teignmouth. And as a finale for this part of the journey west comes the journey alongside the Teign estuary. In contemplative moments, I have often wondered what manner of response there would be if a railway proposed the present route from Exeter to Newton Abbot today. Imagine the clamour and uprising of the planners, conservationists and nimbys. And yet, those very same planners, conservationists and nimbys probably largely love and cherish the creation that the South Devon Railway, unencumbered by the intervention of the forebears of these worthies, fashioned. If I may be allowed a little smile, I have found over the years that one of the best ways of aggravating planners in particular, is to suggest gently that if town and country planning as an industry had existed in past centuries we would be probably be denied the vernacular interest, and beauty, that many of our ancient towns and villages, thank goodness, offer us.

From Newton Abbot we still ascend past Totnes to the track's switchback along the southern slopes of Dartmoor, perhaps remembering the commotion of steam trains as they climbed Dainton to get to Totnes, and then Rattery and Hemerdon banks. The railway in Plymouth is less than it was, but Brunel's Royal Albert Bridge strides across the Tamar as it has done since 1859, even if it has been paralleled for more than fifty years by the much less impressive engineering of the road bridge. We still traverse England's furthest westernmost county by the Cornwall and West Cornwall Railways' serpentine route, surrounded by

Opposite top - On 31 August 1960, the inside of Swindon works played host to both old and new motive power. *Top* - A view of a bay in the erecting shop at Swindon Works. Prominent is "Castle" class 4-6-0 No. 4086 "Builth Castle".

Bottom - "Warship" class B-B diesel hydraulics D869 (later named "Zest") and D829 "Magpie" under construction at Swindon Works.

countryside and the remains of former industrial glory until we reach the very special light of Penzance. The station here, again, is not what it once was, but it still retains its overall roof, and at train times is busy enough.

I mention the very special light of Penzance, because it is not far from there to Newlyn which enraptured (and still enraptures) artists, including from 1885 Stanhope Forbes (1857-1947), who was a member of a diverse and widespread railway dynasty. He was the founding father of the Newlyn School, and whilst he may not have chosen a railway career, as a number of his relatives had, he was not averse to painting railway subjects, including the celebrated work "The Terminus" of 1925, which is a depiction of Penzance Station, and which is now in the care of the National Railway Museum. The railway connection to the artists of Newlyn, Penzance and St Ives was also a practical one. For a number of years a dedicated luggage van was attached to the "Flying Dutchman" express to take canvasses from the Penzance area to the Royal Academy's spring exhibition in London.

We have nearly reached the terminus of this book, but the terminus I wish to end my text with is just a little to the East and North of Penzance. It is, of course, St Ives at the end of the branch from St Erth. Although, of course, I knew of the St Ives line from a long time back, I physically came across it at St Erth only a few years ago, and found it moreover on a glorious sunny day. I parked the car in the spacious car park, wandered into the station, and found myself transported back years, surrounded by Great Western semaphore signals, a proper signal box, a bay platform for the branch, a refreshment room, and much fresh paint and masses of carefully tended flowers. There was also a proper booking office, which boasted pictures, taken by one of its staff, of trains on the mainline. I determined to travel, and

on my next jaunt to the area took the train from Penzance and changed to a two car diesel multiple unit for the short trip.

As is well known, the St Ives branch was the last broad gauge line to open (in 1877), and lived a busy, if fairly unremarkable, life until it was proposed for closure in the Beeching report, but reprieved. Freight ceased in 1966, and St Ives station platform was moved to accommodate car parking in 1971, and it now classed as a "community railway", reflecting its support from the local authority. There can be no doubt that the little four and a quarter mile line gives great benefit to the town of St Ives, which was definitely not designed for the motor car, with good parking facilities at St Erth, and the 1978 station at Lelant Saltings specifically designed for park and ride. The line hugs the coast for virtually its whole route, much of its path being carved out of the cliffs (planners, conservationists and nimbys please, once again, take note) and provides splendid views of the Hayle Estuary, and the beaches fringing St Ives Bay.

Whenever I visit St Ives I always use the railway, revelling in the short ride and the scenery. The pretty town has many attractions, all of which have been catalogued a thousand times, including eating places to cater for every taste. Without denigrating all the other good stuff, my trips tend to involve turning right out of the station and taking a short walk to take a table at a particular restaurant, not so long ago rated by a national newspaper's food critic as being in the top ten in the United Kingdom. The magnificent food here provides a fitting prelude for the eventual return journey on the train. The two brilliant things seem to compensate each other, and long may this remain the *status quo*. What a grand thought to end with. Two of my greatest obsessions – railways and food.

A splendid range of 1950's and 1960's cars provides the foreground for "Hall" class 4-6-0 No 4959 "Purley Hall" as it passes through Maidenhead with a down express freight. 10 March 1961.

57xx class 0-6-0PT No 8770 and 15xx class 0-6-0PT 1504 on station pilot duty simmer gently outside Paddington whilst awaiting work. 2 July 1960.

"Grange" class 4-6-0 No. 6860 "Aberporth Grange" on a down milk empties train at Maidenhead. 10 March 1961.

Tiverton Station, with 1400 class 0-4-2T on the push-pull train from Tiverton Junction and a diesel multiple unit en route from Dulverton to Exeter St Davids. 7 September 1963

End of an era. And full circle from where we came in. Modified Hall 4-6-0 7915 "Mere Hall" at Paddington with the 16.15 to Bicester, the last regular steam working from the station. 17 May 1965.